The Armenian Genocide:
Resisting the Inertia of Indifference

Lorne Shirinian and Alan Whitehorn

Pat,

We remember our ancestral roots, while recognizing we are all sisters + brothers,

with fond wishes,

AW

April 2001.

Other Books from Blue Heron Press

Fiction
Lorne Shirinian, *History of Armenia and Other Fiction*

Poetry
Lorne Shirinian, *Rough Landing*

The Blue Heron Press Anthology: New Voices from Kingston

Cultural Criticism
Lorne Shirinian, *Survivor Memoirs of the Armenian Genocide*

Lorne Shirinian, *Writing Memory: The Search for Home in Armenian Diaspora Literature as Cultural Practice*

Political History
Lorne Shirinian, *Quest for Closure: The Armenian Genocide and the Search for Justice in Canada*

The Armenian Genocide:
Resisting the Inertia of Indifference

Lorne Shirinian and Alan Whitehorn

Blue Heron Press

The Armenian Genocide: Resisting the Inertia of Indifference,
First Canadian Edition,
Blue Heron Press, 160 Greenlees Drive, Kingston, Ontario, Canada K7K 6P4.

"The Armenian Genocide and Its Aftermath: Genocide Denial, A Canadian Perspective" © Lorne Shirinian, 2001

"The Armenian Genocide: A Canadian Perspective," © Alan Whitehorn, 2001

All rights reserved. This may not be produced in whole or in part in any form without permission.

National Library of Canada Cataloguing in Publication Data

Shirinian, Lorne, 1945 –
    The Armenian genocide: resisting the inertia of indifference

1st Canadian ed.
Includes essays, poems and letters
Includes bibliographical references
ISBN 0-920266-24-X

1. Armenian massacres, 1915-1923 – Foreign public opinion, Canadian.
2. Armenian massacres, 1915-1923 – Poetry. I. Whitehorn, Alan. II. Title.

DS195.5.S542 2001   956.6'2015   C2001-930386-6

Cover Art by the Vancouver-based artist, Nora Patrich, titled "Why?"

Table of Contents

Introduction...1

Timeline of the Armenian Genocide...5

The Armenian Genocide: A Canadian Perspective, Alan Whitehorn ...7

The Armenian Genocide and Its Aftermath: Genocide Denial, A Canadian Perspective, Lorne Shirinian ...32

Poems by Lorne Shirinian, from *Earthquake* and *Rough Landing* ...55

Poems by Alan Whitehorn, *Ancestral Voices*...63

Appendix I: Selected headlines in Canadian newspapers on the Armenian Genocide ...74

Appendix II: Statement from the Association of Genocide Scholars ...76

Appendix III: Letter from Alan Whitehorn to the *Globe and Mail*...78

Appendix IV: Letter from Lorne Shirinian to the *Toronto Star*...80

Selected Bibliography on the Armenian Genocide...82

Acknowledgements

An earlier version of "The Armenian Genocide and Its Aftermath: Genocide Denial, A Canadian Perspective" was presented at the Conference on Human Rights Issues in the Eastern Mediterranean and Asia Minor held in Toronto, May 19-21, 2000, sponsored by the Hellenic-Canadian Federation of Ontario.

An earlier version of "The Armenian Genocide: A Canadian Perspective" was presented at the Conference on Human Rights Issues in the Eastern Mediterranean and Asia Minor held in Toronto, May 19-21, 2000, sponsored by the Hellenic-Canadian Federation of Ontario.

Lorne Shirinian dedicates this work
to the Shirinian and the Mazmanian families.

Alan Whitehorn dedicates this work to Siroun Hamamjian

This book is for all those who have suffered
and still suffer from genocide.

Introduction

As relatives of survivors of the Armenian Genocide, we grew up with the terrible stories of slaughter and the miraculous tales of survival of our family members and their friends—fellow orphans and exiles who had also survived the Genocide and had come to Canada to begin new lives in the Armenian diaspora. As we passed through the various stages of our lives, we would share our past, the rich history and culture, and the awful stories of destruction of a people whose nation lay at the crossroads of East and West and thus were the constant victims of conquerors: Persians, Greeks, Romans, Arab, Mongols, and finally the Turks. Each put its mark on Armenians throughout the ages, but none more violently and more definitively than the Ottoman Turks. On April 24, 1915, the Ottoman Turkish government headed by Talaat Pasha, Enver Pasha, and Djemal Pasha, unleashed a premeditated plot to rid the Ottoman Empire of its Armenian citizens.[1] Throughout the Empire except in Constantinople and in Smyrna, where there was a considerable foreign presence of the diplomatic core and commercial interests, Armenians were expelled from their homes and homeland and forced upon the dusty roads without adequate food or shelter, where they were subject to murderers, marauders, soldiers, and the hostile population of Turks and Kurds.[2] Those who survived the death marches ended up in camps in the desert of Der-Zor in what today is Syria, where starvation and disease awaited them. After the war, those who had survived were gathered in refugee camps run by the Red Cross and Near East Relief, whose workers tried desperately to reunite families. It was in these circumstances that our grandparents and parents survived. When Kemal Ataturk began his nationalist war to rid Turkey of foreigners, the Armenian survivors were moved once more to other orphanages in the Middle East and in Greece.

Lorne's father—Mampre Shirinian—was in the Armenian orphanage in Corfu, Greece, when he was randomly chosen to come to Canada by the Armenian Relief Society of Canada in conjunction with the Lord Mayor's Fund of London, England. He, along with 108 other orphans, came to Canada in two groups in 1922 and 1924. They were brought to a Farm Home in Georgetown, Ontario, where they were taught skills in order to become farmers in Southern Ontario. It was at this orphanage that his father met his uncle, who would arrange for his younger sister Mariam Mazmanian, who was in an orphanage in Greece, to come to the farm home. My father and mother, two orphan survivors met and married in 1932. They went to Toronto where they began a business and new lives in Canada. They had two sons, Lorne and George, who are both very active in the field of Armenian studies.

Alan's grandmother—metzmama—was another of the many orphans of the 1915 genocide. As a young homeless child, she was found wandering the streets, not knowing her name or age. Somehow amidst the death and destruction she survived. Those who found her named her Sirhoun (Armenian for beautiful). As a child, Sirhoun spent many long and lonely years in various refugee camps in one country after another. Eventually she was to be shipped with other refugees to America, but en route disembarked in Egypt and was adopted by an Armenian family in the diaspora. Later she married another survivor and soon a child was born—Vartouie (Armenian for Rose). Alan's grandfather, however, could not cope with the horrific memory of the genocide, and committed suicide while his young bride was bearing her second child. Sirhoun was now a young, impoverished widow, but somehow she survived another tragedy. Amidst the devastating conflict of World War II, a Canadian-born Englishman and Armenian woman met in Alexandria, Egypt. It was West meets East. When the war ended, Malcolm and Vartouie went to England. Soon Alan was born, but given the housing shortages and post-war rationing, the family soon emigrated to Canada in the early 1950s, where they have lived ever since.

We both grew up as the inheritors of our families' personal and our nation's collective histories. With this comes the responsibility to try to right the immense wrong that was done to the Armenian nation in 1915. Histories, eye-witness testimonies, government documents, and survivor accounts clearly identify the perpetrator and the victims of genocide. Diplomatic accounts from many European countries and the

United States indicate without doubt that all knew the terrible extent of the human and material destruction. Nevertheless, many governments today—including the Canadian government—have chosen not to acknowledge officially that a genocide took place. Sadly, it seems that commercial interests are a greater priority than any moral imperative. The objective of this book is to sensitize Canadians that a community of their fellow citizens still suffers a great wrong and that it is in the power of our government to help partly heal the terrible wrong by acknowledging the Armenian Genocide, as the government of France has recently done.

The essays we have chosen to include are versions of papers presented at a conference on Human Rights abuses in the Eastern Mediterranean and Asia Minor, held in Toronto on May 19-21, 2000. Our approach and perspective to the Armenian Genocide are distinctly Canadian. In our interdependent and interconnected world, we are increasingly responsible for the way we act towards each other. It is our hope that these essays will bring a greater understanding of human rights issues as they pertain to the Armenian Genocide.

Lorne Shirinian and Alan Whitehorn,
Kingston, Ontario,
April 24, 2001.

Notes

[1] See Vahakn Dadrian, *Warrant for Genocide: Key Elements of Turko-Armenian Conflict* (New Brunswick, New Jersey: Transaction Publishers, 1999) 93-103.

[2] The fate of Smyrna and its Armenian and Greek populations was sealed when in 1922, the nationalist Turkish government of Kemal Ataturk burned the city and killed or expelled its non-Turkish inhabitants. See Marjorie Housepian, *Smyrna 1922: The Destruction of a City* (Kent, Ohio: Kent State University Press, 1988).

Timeline of the Armenian Genocide

In order to place the essays that follow in a clearer context, we offer this timeline of some of the major events leading up to the Genocide and after.

1887: The earliest known Armenian immigrant to Ontario, Garabed Nergararian, who came to Port Hope.

1895-1896: Sultan Abdul Hamid orders the massacres of Armenians. 250,000 Armenians throughout the Ottoman Empire are slaughtered.

1896: The Union and Progress Party (Young Turks) is formed.

1890-1900: The first Armenians arrived in Canada to work in factories in Southern Ontario.

1908: The Turkish Revolution.

1909: Armenians are massacred in Cilicia.

1914-18: World War I.

April 24, 1915: Some 200 Armenian intellectuals and community leaders are rounded up in Constantinople and in other cities. They are deported and killed. This marked the beginning of the Armenian Genocide.

1915-1922: Armenian Genocide. Armenians throughout the Ottoman Empire are deported and exiled from their homes. On the way they are slaughtered en mass. In all, perhaps some 1.5 million Armenians are massacred. The survivors are dispersed throughout the world, never allowed to return to their homes.

1917: Russian Revolution.

May 28, 1918: The creation of the first Republic of Armenia.

1921: The formation of the USSR.

July 1923: The first group of Armenian orphans arrives at the farm home in Georgetown, Ontario.

Sept. 1924: The second group of Armenian orphans arrives in Georgetown.

1952: The Canadian Armenian Congress succeeds in having a less restrictive category applied for the purposes of immigration.

1988: A devastating earthquake in Armenia. Over 25,000 are killed, and many thousands are left homeless.

1991: Armenia declares its independence from Moscow. The new Republic of Armenia is created.

The Armenian Genocide: A Canadian Perspective [1]

Alan Whitehorn

The Term Genocide:[2]

In the 20th century, two new terms were created to portray the political horrors that we have witnessed in the century just ended. These two terms – totalitarianism (1920s) and genocide (1944)[3] sadly are not about democracy and justice, but rather their opposites. It is important to note that often a virulent form of nationalism was a key catalyst in the rise of totalitarianism and genocide.

Nationalism clearly can take many forms, but in the main two major variants can be discerned: 1) an open and tolerant variant (where all of the inhabitants of a particularly territory are deemed to be members, irrespective of religion, race or political creed) or 2) a closed variant where a people are defined exclusively by some demographic trait such as race, religion, or language).[4]

The concept of genocide seems foreign, even remote, to many Canadians. Yet, further historical investigation will reveal the tragic tale of the Beothuk,[5] – a nation/people who no longer exist, but who once inhabited Newfoundland, with the last member dying in 1829. Canadians, should they choose to look, can find examples of genocide in all four corners of the globe.

There are a number of definitions of genocide which exist, but the December 9, 1948 United Nations' International Convention on the Prevention and Punishment of the Crime of Genocide is amongst the most widely cited and outlines the following features:

> 1) killing members of a group;
> 2) causing serious bodily or mental harm to members of a group;
> 3) deliberately inflicting on a group conditions of life calculated to bring about its physical destruction in

whole or in part;
4) imposing measures intended to prevent births within a group;
5) forcibly transferring children of one group to another.[6]

Index and Scale of Ethnic Persecution:

Genocide—the attempt to annihilate an entire people—is the most extreme form of ethnic persecution. But before that level of violence and magnitude of death is pursued, other less sweeping degrees or measures can be employed, often as precursor acts. They might include:

1) state-decreed and enforced assimilation that leads to loss of cultural identity of a collective minority;
2) forced migration or mandatory relocation within a state, often to a more hostile physical environment;
3) forced emigration (i.e. compulsory relocation and exile to a foreign state);
4) ethnic massacres of a local or periodic sort;
5) ethnic cleansing -an attempt to liquidate one group of people from a particular region;
6) genocide -the attempted total annihilation of a particular population that resides within the scope of an entire state.[7]

Past Ethnic Slaughter and Attempted Obliteration of a People/Tribe or Nation:

Sadly, the history of the world is one full of examples of ethnic slaughter and attempted obliteration of a particular people/tribe or nation. Some episodes are of legendry scale, given the final outcome. For example, who has not heard of the destruction of Troy (as portrayed by the Greek playwright Euripides in *The Trojan Women*)? Who does not recall from history classes the military defeat and total destruction of Carthage by the Romans to the point that the lands were to be sown with salt to make the lands uninhabitable for both crops and people? The scale and intensity of the destruction of these two peoples of antiquity were so extensive that it required great efforts even to find the location of the remains of these peoples' homelands.

Importance and Continued Relevance of Topic:

It is tragic and perhaps telling about our modern era that there is little doubt regarding the increased importance of the concept of genocide and related terms such as holocaust, ethnic cleansing,[8] or killing fields. Not only have we created additional terms to describe the horror, we see a proliferation in the number of new books available on the specific case study of the 1915 Armenian genocide. For example the Chapters' web site listed 40 books on the Armenian genocide, including several by my colleague Lorne Shirinian.[9] We also see a proliferation of works written providing a general overview on the topic of genocide in which the Armenian experience is cited as an important case study, along with a growing list of other genocides (e.g. Rwanda).

The Armenian Genocide of 1915:

Sadly because of the passage of almost a century, and other considerations that influence government decision-makers, it is still necessary to establish the basic facts and principles surrounding the genocide of Armenians in 1915.

History of Massacres, Pogroms, Ethnic Cleansing and Genocide:

Alas the history of the Eastern Mediterranean region of the Balkans and the Near East is one in which there are ample examples of ethnic persecution, massacres and even attempted genocide even to this day. Our contemporary newspapers and television newscasts are filled with reports on recent events in Croatia, Bosnia and Herzegovina and Kosovo for which UN peacekeeping troops (e.g. UNPROFOR in Croatia) including Canadians were involved and continue to be at considerable risk.[10] Thus, it is important for our citizenry, government officials and military personnel to learn more about the historic events of this region and the important lessons to apply.

Background Context:

As the expansive multi-national Ottoman Empire collapsed and the smaller and more homogeneous polity of Turkey began to emerge, increasingly Armenians were not one of many ethnic groups in a vast empire, but one of a diminishing and more vulnerable few. These geographic and ethnic demographic changes, along with a growing sense of nationalism, altered the dynamics of how the Turkish political leaders perceived its remaining ethnic minorities.

Ominously in 1895-1896, about 200,000 Armenians were massacred. This was to be, however, just a prelude[11] to the state-decreed forced deportation, starvation, torture and death of hundreds of thousands of Armenians in 1915 that led to the culmination of about one and a half million dead.[12] There are a number of independent and reputable witnesses to this tragic period. Among them are the accounts of Leslie Davis, the US Consul at Karput. His report to the American government included the following account:

> Old men sat there mumbling incoherently. Women with matted hair and sunken eyes sat staring like maniacs. One, whose face has haunted my memory ever since, was so emaciated and the skin was drawn so tightly over her features that her head appeared to be only a lifeless skull. Others in the spasms of death. Children with bloated bellies were on the ground wallowing in filth. Some were in convulsions. All in the camp were beyond help.[13]
>
> A remarkable thing about the bodies that we saw was that nearly all of them were naked. ... There were gaping bayonet wounds on most of the bodies, usually in the abdomen or chest, sometimes in the throat. Few persons had been shot, as bullets were too precious. It was cheaper to kill with bayonets and knives. Another remarkable thing was that nearly all the women lay flat

on their back and showed signs of barbarous mutilation by the bayonets of the gendarmes, these wounds would have been inflicted in many cases probably after the women were dead. We also noticed that all the bodies in these valleys were apparently those of people who had been on the road at least one or two months, ... from distant places.

We estimated that in the course of our ride around the lake, and actually within the space of twenty-four hours, we had seen the remains of not less than ten thousand Armenians who had been killed around Lake Goeljuk.[14]

In addition to the torture, starvation, disease, and death, homes were confiscated, property stolen, and churches and grave sites destroyed. More importantly and traumatically, a generation of children were killed or orphaned. An entire people were at peril–that is to say they were the victims of genocide. These criteria (e.g. forced migration, stripping of property, denial of food and medical services, torture, destruction of cultural sites and ethnic massacres) are incorporated into the definition of genocide subsequently outlined by the United Nations in 1948 in the aftermath of World War II. Sadly, several of the traits of genocide, the repeated denial of the genocide[15] and the Turkish state's overseeing the deterioration and disappearance of Armenian cultural sites in the region continues to this day. This is a form of cultural genocide[16] in the contemporary era that reinforces the wrongs of an earlier era and adds insult to injury.

Today the harsh demographic reality is that vastly more Armenians live in the North American portion of the Diaspora than in their ancestral homelands in Turkey.[17] There is a tragic parallel to the plight of Jews in Germany and Poland.[18] In a very crude statistical sense, both genocides "succeeded" at one brutal level; they successfully depopulated a significant ethnic group from an original ancestral homeland. A vast portion of an entire generation died and the rest had to choose involuntary exile. Sadly, the 1915 genocide also "succeeded" in another sense. During WWI and the 1920s, the state-sponsored deportations and appalling ethnic massacres [19]were the topic of numerous newspaper editorials[20] and classroom discussion. However, with the passage of almost a century, a significant number of Canadians do not know about the historical fact of the genocide or, in the case of some government officials, do not wish to publicly declare the existence of a genocide for which there is so much historical evidence, lest they adversely affect matters of commerce (e.g. potential Candu nuclear reactor sales)[21] or military alliance (i.e. NATO) relations with a key and strategically-situated member state.

Documentation:

When the question of genocide is raised, a number of techniques of analysis are possible. The most poignant and moving is the highly personal accounts of the victims who survived. Survival, of course, is problematic on the genocide question, particularly the more "successful" the genocide is. How many and who survive are key questions affecting the information and documentation received. Of course, some, particularly those accused, will object and suggest that a victim is not an ideal witness to a crime, whether domestic or international. Certainly, the traumatic effects of torture, rape, murder and genocide can greatly affect one's outlook and ability to "share" the experience with others. Nevertheless, the human spirit is capable of enduring much and memories sometimes recall great detail. Ideally, oral accounts are eventually recorded. We thus have examples from around the world of survivor's memoirs. (Perhaps the most notable genocide memoir of the 20th century was the diary of a young Jewish non-survivor of the Holocaust -- Anne Frank.) Amongst the Canadian published or authored autobiographies or biographies of victims of the 1915 Armenian genocide are: D. Sakayan, *An Armenian Doctor in Turkey –Grabed Hatcherian: My Smyrna Ordeal of 1922* (Montreal, Orod, 1997); L. Shirinian, *Survivor Memoirs of the Armenian Genocide* (Reading, Taderon, 1999) and L. Shirinian, *Quest for Closure* (Kingston, Blue Heron, 1999).

In addition to victim's testimony, both domestic and international courts often look for external validation from independent third parties or neutral observers. Since the American Government was neutral for most of the war, its officials had more scope than some other governments for placing officials in the field who could send back detailed reports. Amongst the more accessible and frequently cited works are the American Ambassador to Turkey, Henry Morgenthau's autobiography entitled *Ambassador Morgenthau's Story* (Garden City, Doubleday, Page, 1919) and US Consul Leslie Davis report to the

American government, reprinted in "American Consul's Report" in S. Blair, *The Slaughterhouse Province* pp. 82-87 in V. Dadrian, ed., *The Ottoman Empire: A Troubled Legacy – Views, Comments and Judgments by Noted Experts Worldwide* (Association of Genocide Scholars, Zoryan, Cambridge, 1997).

People of non-Turkish or non-Armenian background were in some ways also "independent" in that they were neither the victim nor the victimizer. Amongst the most famous works published in English are those associated with the British Government's Blue Book – Viscount Bryce, *The Treatment of Armenians in the Ottoman Empire 1915-16* (London, [British Government], 1916) (documents compiled by Arnold Toynbee). One of the key researchers went on to publish many other books including Arnold Toynbee, *Armenian Atrocities: The Murder of a Nation* (London, Hodder and Stoughton, 1915). Turkey's ally in WWI was Germany, but the country was not without its witnesses of genocide. One of the most widely quoted and cited was the German missionary Dr. Johannes Lepsius in his books *Deutschland und Armenien 1914-1918 Sammlung diplomatischer Aktenstucke* (Potsdam, Temperlverlag, 1919) and *Le Rapport secret sur les massacres d'Arménie* (1916).

In more recent decades, there has been a growth in the study of comparative sociology and comparative politics. The topic of genocide is one area of growing comparison, both analytically and empirically. Interestingly, all of the major theoretical works in English on genocide include the Armenian case study. For example, we can note the following works:

from the United States:
I. Horowitz, *Taking Lives: Genocide and State Power* (New Brunswick, Transaction, 1980, 3rd edition). This enduring book has gone through three editions.

from South Africa:
L. Kuper, *Genocide* (Harmondsworth, Penguin, 1981)

From Israel:
Israel W. Charny, *How Can We Commit the Unthinkable: Genocide the Human Cancer* (Westview, Boulder, 1982).

from Canada:
F. Chalk and K. Jonassohn, *The History and Sociology of Genocide: Analyses and Case Studies* (New Haven, Yale, 1990).

Comparison can be more specific and we often find there is offered a comparison of the two key case studies of genocide in the 20th century—the Jewish Holocaust which occurred during WWII and its antecedent the Armenian genocide which occurred in WWI. Amongst the works with this focus are I. Horowitz, *Taking Lives: Genocide and State Power*; V. Dadrian, "The Historical and Legal Interconnections Between the Armenian Genocide and the Jewish Holocaust: From Impunity to Restributive Justice", *Yale Jounral of International Law* (Volume 23, #2, Summer 1998); R. Melson, *Revolution and Genocide: On the Origins of the Armenian Genocide and the Holocaust* Chicago, University of Chicago, 1992) and R. Melson, "Provocation or Nationalism: A Critical Enquiry into the Armenian Genocide of 1915" in R. Hovannisian, ed., *The Armenian Genocide in Perspective* (also reprinted in Chalk and Jonassohn *The History and Sociology of Genocide*).

Lastly, less scholarly, but still highly germane, are the daily press reports from the era. Here we can, as I have done, go through the back issues of Canadian newspapers on microfilm for the germane period, particularly 1915, or we can read compendiums of newspaper articles such as the following:

Le Genocide Armenien dans la Presse Canadienne/The Armenian Genocide in the Canadian Press Volume I, 1915-1916 (Montreal, Armenian National Committee of Canada, 1985) and
Le Genocide Armenien dans la Presse Canadienne/The Armenian Genocide in the Canadian Press Volume II, 1916-1923 (n.l., Armenian National Committee of Canada, n.d.).

Together these writings (memoirs, biographies, case studies, comparative analyses and press accounts) provide a comprehensive and in-depth account of genocide.

Attitude of Subsequent Governments of the Genocide Protagonist:

The attitude of subsequent governments of the genocide protagonist can be a major assistance or obstacle in addressing the issue of punishment of the genocide perpetrators, redress for the victims and their families or emotional closure for subsequent generations.[22] Here the contrast between Germany and Turkey in dealing with their respective genocide's responsibility is striking.

What made international and Canadian recognition and continued awareness of the Jewish Holocaust easier was in part the attitude of post-War German governments. Germany, having been defeated in WWII, was a country[23] occupied by the victorious Allies and was forced to confront its past acts of inhumanity and genocide. The Allied-imposed Nuremberg Trials were landmark cases in international criminal law[24] and prepared the way for the UN Declaration on Genocide in 1948. Over time a former authoritarian and totalitarian state succeeded dramatically in the democratization of its domestic political culture and became one of Europe's most successful democracies. For example, its has scored very well (97% for West Germany in the 1980s and 98% for all of Germany in the 1990s) on the widely-used Human Rights index.[25] A democratic and pluralistic culture has made it easier for German governments to acknowledge their past genocidal deeds and openly respond to claims of redress from the victims.

In contrast to German actions in the post-war era, Turkey, in the main, was more successful in resisting post-WWI efforts at occupation and intervention by European powers. As a result, it was not forced by foreign powers to deal in any sustained major way with its past genocidal deeds, nor did it foster a flourishing democratic and pluralistic culture.[26] Right up to the contemporary era, Turkish politics have been characterized by political repression, censorship, banning of political parties, and military coups or threats of military intervention.[27] For example, Turkey's human rights index (with regard to both individuals and ethnic groups) has generally been poor and the country's score was only 41% in 1986 (below the world average of 55%) and, while slightly better at 44% in 1991 was even further below the world average of 62%.[28] Turkey's human rights record is quite poor for a NATO country and is a major factor in Turkey's lack of success in gaining full entry into the European community. Given the prevailing authoritarian culture in Turkey during the twentieth century, it perhaps should not be surprising that successive Turkish governments have continued to deny the historic record of the genocide of its Armenian population. What is quite unexpected, if not disquieting, is that recent Canadian governments seem to have been acquiescent to Turkey's official position regarding the denial of one of the most important genocides of the twentieth century.[29] This is a theme to which we will return later in this chapter.

One ray of hope on the Turkish domestic front is that with increased emigration (and contact with other cultures), greater public access (e.g. through the Internet) to more diverse information, and with the passage of time, it is more likely that a new generation willing to challenge the wall of genocidal denial (e.g. The Turkish researcher, Taner Akçam) will emerge to foster the path of greater academic freedom, democratization, and the emergence of a civil society.[30]

If the actions of genocide denial by the Turkish state have been a hindrance to presenting the Armenian case of genocide, so to has been the absence of an independent and democratic Armenian state. Both Tsarist imperialism and Soviet expansionism meant that for most of the 20th century there was no independent Armenian state to promote the cause of the genocide victims. A nominally autonomous Armenian republic within the former Soviet Union, and under the firm hand of the Russian-dominated government in Moscow, had little latitude to push the Armenian genocide issue. But now with an independent, albeit a vulnerable land-locked state, the Armenian government can be a clear and persistent voice lobbying Canada and the world to remember the genocide and to persuade Turkey to do likewise. Time will tell if such a voice will make a difference.

Perceptions and Feelings Towards Armenians and Ottoman Empire/Turkey:

In any complex triangle of relationships, the perceptions of one party are partially influenced by the perception of another. The Canadian government's and public's view of Armenians has never been in isolation of its opinions on the Ottoman Empire/Turkey or the general picture of international relations at a particular time. For example, during WWI the Ottoman Empire was perceived as an enemy, whereas during WWII it was a "neutral", and during the Cold War from 1945 to 1990 it was seen as an important and geo-strategic ally. Thus it was easier for Canadians to criticize the Ottoman regime during WWI and its aftermath than during the Cold War when the West's need for the support of Turkey in a key strategic region was pivotal.

Human Rights and Big Power Geopolitics:

In the first part of the 20th century the pursuit of the interests of the British Empire (which included Canada) affected the willingness to promote the Armenian cause. In the second half of the 20th century the interests of fostering first the US alliance system (which included Canada) amidst the Cold War against the Soviet Union, and secondly promoting American interests in the volatile region of the Middle East affected the willingness to raise the Armenian question. That being said, we have had and continue to have some autonomy in foreign affairs, particularly on the issue of human rights. Within the general alliance parameters and condition of international affairs, there were, nevertheless, specific perceptions that Canadians showed towards Armenians and the 1915 genocide. The first was that of initial shock and profound outrage that fellow Christians were being slaughtered. Later despite restrictive immigration policy towards non-Europeans in the 1920s, some orphans (but not many compared to the numbers homeless) were brought to Canada (most notably the Georgetown Boys of Southern Ontario). However, it was expected that these young orphans would be assimilated into Canadian life. Despite shocking revelations about the genocidal atrocities in the Nazi concentration camps, the Cold War with the Soviet Union was at its peak in the 1950s. Accordingly, Turkey was an extremely valuable ally, and this meant that the topic of the Armenian genocide was "inopportune." The 1960s was marked by an opening up of Canada's immigration policy to a greater variety of immigrants (including a wave of Armenian immigrants not so much from their original homeland in Turkey but from the Diaspora, particularly the Middle East), a government policy of multiculturalism and the beginnings of detente. The histories of the ethnic minorities in Canada mushroomed and the questioning of Turkey's human rights policies, both in the present and the past, was easier to raise in an age of lessening superpower tensions. But when acts of violence against Turkish officials by Armenian revolutionary nationalists took place in Canada, the Canadian public's reaction was one of shock and condemnation. The concern about Islamic fundamentalism in the Middle East, the 1990 Gulf War, and wariness about the future intentions of Russia continue to make

Turkey a key geo-political ally of the United States and Canada and thus increase the likelihood of Ottawa not wishing to unnecessarily alienate Turkey by raising the issue of a genocide almost a century old.

Canadian Perceptions:

Of course no modern society is monolithic and a country as large, heterogeneous and pluralistic as Canada is bound to reflect differences of opinion and perspectives. Even when we look at Canadian perceptions of the Armenian genocide of 1915, we hear a number of distinct voices. There are, of course, the official Canadian government statements through the Prime Minister and the Governor General.[31] There are also the more specific comments in the House of Commons by MPs, both on the government side and that of the opposition parties (e.g. House of Commons debate on February 15, 1999).[32] There are also the announcements by officials from various government departments primarily from the Department of External Affairs/Foreign Affairs, but at times by the Justice Department, Ministry of Trade, and Ministry of National Defence. The members of the media are key gatekeepers determining what stories and letters to the editor get printed (note for example the debate in the letters to the editor in the Toronto *Globe and Mail* in July 1999). Newspaper editors and television news directors decide what prominence and balance, if any, a topic such as genocide is given.

The public at large can provide input, depending on the general knowledge level of the issue and the intensity of feelings on the subject. However, public opinion surveys reveal that most Canadians know relatively little about foreign affairs, and in general, even less about events overseas almost a century ago. Of course, there are exceptions in our multi-cultural society. Some ethnic groups in Canada may have a great deal more knowledge and stronger feelings on a particular subject. Thus for example, the Armenians, Greeks and Jews in Canada are likely to have strong views on the topic of either genocide in general or the suffering of ethnic minorities under the hands of the Ottoman Empire or Turkish government. One suspects it is no accident that two of the Liberal MPs most vocal in a positive fashion on this issue (Jim Karygiannis and Sarkis Assadourian) have done so in part due to their ethnic roots. By contrast, members of the Turkish community in Canada, along with the Turkish Embassy staff, have been vocal on the other side claiming no genocide of Armenians occurred in 1915.[33]

In addition to members of interested ethnic communities in Canada, other groups may also become involved on the genocide issue ranging from humanitarian groups such as Amnesty International and Human Rights Watch. Certainly during the WWI years and 1920s, church groups were active with relief efforts,[34] and raised the public's awareness. Even though genocide is an issue of profound moral implications, commercial corporations can have some, albeit indirect, interest in the subject. In as much as preoccupation with the issue of genocide may lead to a Turkish government backlash, it might adversely affect sales, trade and profits. Thus corporate executives concerned about jeopardizing potential commercial sales (e.g. potential Candu reactor sales) to the Turkish government or business have lobbied to lessen the government's public pronouncements on the genocide issue.[35] This is not the first time, nor is it likely to be the last that debates between profits and morality occur.

Even within a government, there may be disagreement on differing priorities at any particular time. Should the government's priority be to maintain good relations with Turkey, a fellow member state in Canada's key military alliance of NATO? Should the government assist to maximize Canadian exports to all parts of the world, irrespective of another country's human rights record?[36] Should a party in power, such as the Liberal Party, which receives about half of its finances for corporate donations[37], respond favourably to corporate executives' wishes to not provoke a backlash from Turkish authorities? On the other side of the equation, some members of the government (e.g. human rights lawyers in the Justice Department) may be more concerned with Canada's distinguished reputation on international human rights. Is the failure to formally acknowledge one of the world's largest genocides of the 20th century likely to damage Canada's credibility in the field of international human rights and lessen the likelihood of prosecution of those who have committed war crimes?[38] Clearly, a government in a democracy such as Canada must always weigh the balance on both sides of the political ledger (e.g. potential jobs in a key sector or region vs. potential injustice to a particular ethnic group). The world of politics is filled with a mixture of realism and idealism and the Canadian government is no exception in this regard. But there are times when the magnitude of the international crime is so great that morality should prevail. As the Honourable Ed Broadbent, former Director of the Montreal-based International Centre for Human Rights and Democratic Development suggests "When the evidence supporting clear and systematic violation of the most serious of human rights is known and available, surely pragmatic self-interest which is otherwise a norm of foreign policy, must be pushed aside."[39]

One important new variant in the Canadian debate on the topic of genocide is the growing number of Canadian military personnel from the Department of National Defence who have served as international peacekeepers around the world. Increasingly, they have often witnessed horrific scenes of ethnic killing and even genocide from the Balkans to Rwanda. Perhaps most notable in recent years is General Dallaire who served with the United Nations in Rwanda. There is no doubt that he has been profoundly affected by his traumatic experiences of witnessing a genocide in progress that he tried unsuccessfully to stop. His life, his health, and his career have been irrevocably altered by the searing images.[40] General Dallaire has become a powerfully moving voice within the Canadian Armed Forces and amongst Canadians on the topic of genocide and human rights. His voice adds moral weight and echoes the haunting voices (diplomatic, military, and missionary) from the past who likewise were witnesses to an earlier genocide in 1915. Clearly, lessons from the past are still timely today.

Canadian Media:

It should be noted that often in the Canadian media newspaper editors and television news directors have a propensity to seek contrasting viewpoints (particularly television) to provide drama (irrespective of the historical accuracy, the moral validity or the size of the community represented in the contrasting views). This quest for so-called "journalistic balance" is even more so when the younger generation of key media gatekeepers are uncertain about the historical events in question. The 1915 genocide took place long ago, too few know the details or understand the complex history of the region or the dynamics of the debate on the topic (e.g. systematic state denial by the Turkish government and attempt at revisionism).

Clearly, it is imperative to better inform a younger generation of the media and remind them not only of the great importance of a major genocide of the 20th century, but also to point out the contemporary relevance in the comparative study of genocide[41] and the promotion of human rights around the world.[42] In the meantime, we can observe the continued attempts to influence media awareness and the portrayal of the 1915 genocide. These can be seen in the ongoing debate in the press, which sometimes spills over into the unpublished realm. For example, I note one such recent episode in the Canadian media war.

In June and July of 1999 several letters appeared in the Toronto *Globe and Mail* in response to an original article by Alan Freeman: the first letter was on June 26 by Ali Savut, First Counsellor at the Turkish Embassy in Ottawa. That was then followed by a letter dated July 7 from a Vancouver reader Diran Horazian pointing out details of the 1915 genocide, and to which Ehran Ogut, the Turkish Ambassador responded by categorically denying such a genocide. Believing that some Canadian archival information might be helpful, I sent a letter dated July 24 based on extensive academic research of the headlines relating to Armenians in the old Toronto *Globe* for the entire year of 1915.[43] I thought the documentary letter might be informative and helpful to Canadians and government officials engaged in debate on the topic. The responses that I received, while not published in the *Globe and Mail*, were quite varied and, I believe, greatly revealing. One was yet another letter from Ali Savut, First Counsellor at the Turkish Embassy in Ottawa dated August 12 where he suggested my archival research was an "unfair interpretation" and that so-called "impartial historians" suggest another story. The *Globe* chose not to publish the letter, but it was, nevertheless, faxed and hand-delivered to me. Another letter was sent to me in a more personal manner in the form of a hand-written note from an elderly Armenian man in Toronto. In that letter he wrote, "Your integrity in the pursuit of truth and unbiased opinion is appreciated. I commend you for your courage and scholarly approach and attitude. You have my respect and admiration for spreading the truth in a world that ignores truth for political considerations." He then added in a postscript: "I am a survivor of the Armenian genocide perpetrated by the Turks in 1915. I am 92 years old. I pray and hope that I see the day when justice will be done and all my family members along with the almost 2 million martyrs of my nation will finally rest in peace."

Related to this, earlier in the year in response to comments by a government M.P. during the February 15, 1999 Parliamentary debate on the issue of the Armenian genocide, I had sent a similar letter to a senior cabinet minister listing the archival headlines from the old Toronto *Globe*. I received a reply dated April 26, 1999 from the Honourable David Collenette, a Toronto Liberal M.P. and cabinet minister, a close advisor to the Prime Minister and a personal friend of mine from our university days. In that letter he wrote "The Government of Canada acknowledges and deplores the fact that a large number of Armenians and members of other groups lost their lives during the wars that marked the end of the Ottoman Empire. Millions were forcefully displaced in extremely difficult conditions, a situation that gave rise to a large number of deaths and indescribable suffering. Canada feels compassion for the victims of this turbulent period of history...."

What these letters indicate is an ongoing debate between two unequal protagonists (the Turkish government and the few surviving victims), almost a century after the terrible deeds. Alas, we witness another chapter in a sad tale: a foreign government still engaged in denial and an aging victim still appealing for justice. To this debate, we can add the current Canadian government's unwillingness to use the widely-applied term of "genocide." And despite a multitude of archival documents and books on the catastrophic events of 1915, the Canadian government hints at some uncertainty about the scholarly evidence with the phrase "Historians continue to study this dark period of history so that the lessons that can be learned from these events benefit present and future generations." One is left to ask: How much archival evidence?[44] How many books on the case study? How many comparative volumes on genocide are needed to finally acknowledge the dreadful deeds?

Formal Government Declaration:

In contrast to the Canadian government's equivocation, we note the following formal statement by the American President Bill Clinton:

> This week [of April 24] marks the commemoration of one of the saddest chapters of this [the 20th] century: the deportations and massacres of one and a half million Armenians in the closing years of the Ottoman Empire. We join with Armenian-Americans across the nation and with the Armenian community abroad to mourn the loss of so many innocent lives. Today against the background of events in Kosovo, all

| NAME |
| NOM |

ADDRESS
ADRESSE

CITY/PROV.
VILLE/PROV.

POSTAL CODE   TEL.
CODE POSTAL   TEL.
1110 BS013408

ONTARIO LOTTERY CORPORATION (OLC)
CHECK YOUR SELECTIONS FOR ACCURACY.
Rules and other information which regulate all aspects of this lottery game, including limitations of liability and requirements for prize entitlement, are available upon request. The information recorded in the online system takes precedence over information recorded on the ticket, validation slip or selection slip. In communicating information regarding any lottery game to a player, a retailer is deemed to be acting on behalf of the player.

TO CLAIM YOUR PRIZE:
Complete below and keep copy of front.
Prizes under $300 may be claimed from an on-line retailer authorized for this product. Prizes under $50,000 send ticket to: P.O. Box 877, Sault Ste. Marie, ON P6A 5N5. All prizes major (and prizes of $50,000 and over must) be claimed in person at the OLC Prize Office, 33 Bloor Street East, Toronto. Proof(s) of identification may be required for all claims.
Prizes must be claimed by the lawful bearer within twelve months following the draw date.

SOCIÉTÉ DES LOTERIES DE L'ONTARIO (SLO)
VÉRIFIEZ L'EXACTITUDE DE VOS SÉLECTIONS.
On peut se faire communiquer, sur demande les règlements et autres renseignements régissant tous les aspects de ce jeu de loterie, y compris les limitations de responsabilité et les conditions d'obtention des lots. Les renseignements enregistrés dans le système à accès direct l'emportent sur les renseignements portés sur le billet, le coupon de validation ou la fiche de sélection. Pour toutes les communications avec les joueurs au sujet des jeux de loteries, les détaillants sont considérés comme des agents des joueurs.

POUR RÉCLAMER VOTRE LOT.
Remplir la section ci-dessous et garder une photocopie du devant du billet.
Les lots de moins de 300 $ peuvent être perçus chez un détaillant muni d'un terminal autorisé à vendre les billets de ce produit. Pour les lots de moins de 50 000 $, envoyer votre billet à : C.P. 877, Sault Ste. Marie (ON) P6A 5N5. Tous les lots doivent (et les lots de 50 000 $ et plus doivent) être perçus en vous présentant au Bureau des prix de la SLO au 33, rue Bloor est, Toronto. Une preuve d'identité peut être demandée pour toute réclamation.
Tous les lots doivent être réclamés par le porteur légitime du billet dans les douze mois suivant la date du tirage.

NAME
NOM

ADDRESS
ADRESSE

CITY/PROV.
VILLE/PROV.

POSTAL CODE   TEL

LOTTO 6/49
QUICK PICK/MISE-ÉCLAIR
21 APR/AVR 01

```
03 12 16 27 48 49
28 33 36 37 40 42
```

ENCORE 339944
NOT ENTERED / NON-INSCRIT

$ 2.00
000890   013633
8195-0925-5428-0652

TONIGHT'S SUPER 7
$10,000,000
GET YOUR TICKETS NOW!
LOTTO SUPER 7 - CE SOIR
10 000 000 $
ACHETEZ VOS BILLETS!

Americans should recommit themselves to building a world where such events never occur again.[45]

It is not often that I am ashamed of my government in comparison to other states, but this is sadly one such occasion. I am greatly troubled that my government, an early and influential signatory to the United Nations and its principles of human rights[46] has not more clearly and firmly acknowledged a past terrible deed of genocide. Time is running short; only a few survivors of the 1915 genocide remain. This generation lives in a global village where human beings are increasingly interconnected by the internet, television, and airplanes. Political turmoil, genocide, and war in one part of the globe inevitably affect elsewhere. Accordingly, we must speak up regarding both human rights abuses and genocide wherever they occur. The Honourable Ed Broadbent has pointed out that in order for the Canadian government to have credibility on these issues, it cannot deny a major past genocide for the sake of trade, for to do so erodes one of the key foundations of our moral stand against contemporary genocide and ethnic cleansing.

From Genocide to Ethnic Cleansing: Some Lessons for Canadians:

As a Canadian citizen and a professor of political science at the Royal Military College of Canada, I offer the following counsel: If it is deemed morally necessary to send dedicated and brave Canadian peacekeepers abroad to be in harm's way in an effort to try to stop ethnic slaughter and genocide in diverse locales around the globe, then surely it is incumbent upon the Canadian government not to undermine the moral and logical basis of these important commitments of our citizen/soldiers. We cannot and should not put forward two morally contradictory statements: 1) that human rights of an ethnic people matter today and genocide must be stopped even at the risk to Canadian lives; while also saying 2) that human rights of an ethnic people did not matter in the past and we should forget history and focus instead on new trade deals with government's who engage in genocide denial. To allow the latter position to prevail profoundly undercuts our moral and human commitment to peacekeeping and international law. We should not say one genocide counts, while another does not.[47] We either are a world where each individual and each ethnic group have human rights as enunciated in the UN Charter, the UN Declaration of Human Rights and the UN International Convention on the Prevention and Punishment of the Crime of Genocide. Or these principles do not yet prevail and the vision of justice and equality within the world community remain unfulfilled.

The Canadian Government's Conundrum:

Canada has played an important historic role in the promotion of international human rights from the pioneering and key work of McGill academic John Humphrey, the drafter of the UN's 1948 declaration to the contribution to the UN's peacekeeping in East Timor, Rwanda, Croatia, and most recently Kosovo. However, one is left with a profoundly troubling question as one ponders our dedicated peacekeepers in dangerous locales. Is there an undercutting of the logic and morality of their deeds when we ignore or deny older, but precedent-setting cases[48] such as the 1915 genocide of Armenians? Without a doubt, we owe it to acknowledge the moral and political impact of the 1915 genocide to the survivors and their descendants. But as more of our citizen/soldiers serve to protect world peace and human rights, we should not deny the reality and legitimacy of the increasing human psychological toll of our peacekeepers. Nor should we belittle or deny what General Dallaire and his fellow soldiers have witnessed and continue to endure.[49] Genocide has many victims. Not all of them lay strewn on the killing fields. Some return home to Canada as our citizens.

Towards Reconciliation?

The first and natural response of the victims is that of revenge or punishment. But at some point, that is not enough. As in the case of Germany and the Holocaust, we know that we must also build for a more democratic and just future. But how do we travel the long voyage from revenge and punishment to forgiveness?[50] One who has wrestled with this moral dilemma and perhaps can offer a clue is the powerful yet gentle voice of Joy Kogawa. She is a Vancouver-born Japanese-Canadian novelist, who as a child was forcibly deported and interned during WWII. The traumatic experience profoundly shaped her life and her identity. As an adult, she was active in the Japanese Canadian redress movement, but also became involved in a wide range of social justice issues. Here is her counsel on the Armenian genocide:

> There can be no healing without truth telling. There can be no hint of a first step towards reconciliation without acknowledgement of crimes done. When unspeakable horrors against a people are buried, the poison seeps down through generation upon generation. We are witness today that memory cannot be obliterated by time, denial or suppression, and that violence and hatred and cycles of violence continue.[51]

Thus, a clear precondition for any possible reconciliation or forgiveness is the acknowledgement of the deeds by the government (or its heirs) that inflicted the genocide.[52] There too must be some sign of remorse by such a government, and at the very least, some symbolic form of reparations (perhaps a token sum for Armenian cultural libraries, museums, churches, conferences, or books). As a necessary first step, there must emerge a new and open attitude to fostering democratic dialogue between the different fragments of the former Ottoman Empire. At the dawn of the 21st century, there are already some rays of hope. Some citizens and academics from Turkey have begun to speak and establish the first ongoing contacts with their ancestral counterparts.[53] It is a long journey to recognize the brotherhood of man. As J.S. Woodsworth, one of Canada's most famous clergymen turned politician[54] counselled: To begin we must resist the sin of indifference.

We must remember.
 Remember and learn.
Remember and tell.
But also remember and live.
And some day, remember and forgive.

Notes

[1] The ideas expressed in this paper reflect those of the author and not necessarily those of the Government of Canada or the Department of National Defence.

[2] I wish to acknowledge with much gratitude the generous access to the extensive historical research by Lorne Shirinian that has helped the author write this chapter.

[3] R. Lemkin, *Axis Rule in Occupied Europe* (Washington, Carnegie Endowment for International Peace, 1944); see also L. Shirinian, *Quest for Closure: The Armenian Genocide and the Search for Justice in Canada* (Kingston, Blue Heron Press, 1999) p. 146. The originator of the term genocide, Raphael Lemkin is said to have been profoundly influenced by the example of the Armenian case and the gap in international criminal law. See J. Tashjian, "Genocide, the United Nations and the Armenians, in J. Porter, ed., *Genocide and Human Rights: A Global Anthology* (Washington, University Press of America, 1982).

[4] A number of the following variables are often germane in the fostering of nationalist sentiment: a common descent (from the same family roots); common language or alphabet; a common religion; common habits, customs, culture, traditions or values; a contiguous territory (cluster together); and the establishment of a shared political entity. The first three are more exclusionary while the latter three are less so.

[5] These aboriginal people living on the island of Newfoundland painted their faces with red ochre paint and were the source of the term "Red Indian" when European sailors first encountered them. See J. Tuck, "Beothuk" in *The Canadian Encyclopedia* (McClelland and Stewart, Toronto, 1999).

[6] UN General Assembly Resolution 260 A (III) "International Convention on the Prevention and Punishment of the Crime of Genocide" cited in M. Lippman, "Genocide" in M. Bassiouni, ed., *International Criminal Law* (Ardsley, Transaction, 1999, 2nd edition) Volume 1, pp. 595, 597.

[7] See also A. Bell-Fialkoff, *Ethnic Cleansing* (St. Martin's Grifin, N.Y., 1999) p.4 regarding his outline of a population removal index.

[8] See A. Bell-Fialkoff, *Ethnic Cleansing* and V. Volkan, *Blood Lines: From Ethnic Pride to Ethnic Terrorism* (Boulder, Westview, 1997).

[9] V. Dadrian, *The History of the Armenian Genocide: Ethnic Conflict from the Balkans to Anatolia to the Caucasus* (Providence, Berghahn, 1995); R. Hovannisian, ed., *Remembrance and Denial: The Case of the Armenian Genocide* (Detroit, Wayne State, 1999); R. Melson, *Revolution and Genocide: On the Origins of the Armenian Genocide and the Holocaust* (Chicago, University of Chicago Press, 1996); L. Shrinian, *The Impact of the Armenian*

Genocide: Eighty-three Years of Survival and Memory in the Armenian Diaspora (Toronto, University of Toronto, 1998); H. Vassilian, *Armenian Genocide: A Comprehensive Bibliography and Library Resource Guide* (Glendale, Armenian Reference Books Company, 1992); R. Hovannisian, ed., *The Armenian Genocide in Perspective* (New Brunswick, Transaction, 1986); Y. Ternon, *The Armenians: History of a Genocide* (Delmar, Caravan, 1990); L. Shirinian, *Survivor Memoirs of the Armenian Genocide* (Reading, Taderon Press, 1998); A. Sarafian, *United States Official Documents on the Armenian Genocide* (Watertown, Armenian Review, 1998);. A. Sarafian, *United States Official Documents on the Armenian Genocide, Volume 5 Ambassador Morgenthau's Reports* (Watertown, Armenian Review, 1970); L. Davis, S. Blair, *The Slaughterhouse Province: An American Diplomat's Report on the Armenian Genocide of 1915-17* (New Rochelle, Aristide D. Caratzas, 1989); Permanent Peoples Tribunal Staff, *A Crime of Silence: The Armenian Genocide* (N.Y., St. Martin's Press, 1985); V. Dadrian, *Warrant for Genocide* (New Brunswick, Transaction, 1999); R. Hovannisian, ed., *The Armenian Genocide* (N.Y., St. Martin's Press, 1985); Zoryan Institute, *Problems of Genocide* (Toronto, Zoryan, 1997). See also the Indigo web site.

[10] Human Rights Watch, *The Lost Agenda: Human Rights and U.N. Field Operations* (Human Rights Watch, N.Y., 1993)

[11] See L. Etmekjian, "Toynbee, Turks, and Armenians" in *The Armenian Review* (Autumn 1984).

[12] See B. Lewis, *The Emergence of Modern Turkey* (London, Oxford, 1961) p. 350 where he uses the word "holocaust"; A. Toynbee, *Experiences* (N.Y. Oxford, 1969) on pp. 241 and 341 uses the word "genocide"; and Lord Kinross, *The Ottoman Centuries: The Rise and Fall of the Turkish Empire* (N.Y., Morrow Quill, 1977) p. 607; H. Morgenthau, *Ambassador Morgenthau's Story* (Garden City, Doubleday, Page, 1919) p. 322; David Lloyd George, *Memoirs of the Peace Conference* (New Haven, Yale, 1939) Volume 2, p. 62 regarding the magnitude of the number of deaths.

[13] L. Davis "American Consul's Report" in S. Blair, *The Slaughterhouse Province: An American Diplomat's Report on the Armenian Genocide, 1915-1917* (New Rochelle, Aristide D. Caratzas, 1989) p. 76 cited in L. Shirinian, *Quest for Closure*, p. 43

[14] L. Davis "American Consul's Report" in S. Blair, *The Slaughterhouse Province* pp. 82-87 in V. Dadrian, ed., *The Ottoman Empire: A Troubled Legacy – Views, Comments and Judgments by Noted Experts Worldwide* (Association of Genocide Scholars, Zoryan, Cambridge, 1997). For another first hand report by a German war nurse see the passages of Armin Wegner also in the Dadrian compendium, pp. 50-51. See also *AIM* magazine, April, 2000, p. 59.

[15] V. Dadrian, *The Key Elements in the Turkish Denial of the Armenian Genocide: A Case Study of Distortion and Falsification* (Toronto, Zoryan,

1999). One notable exception is that of Taner Akcam, "The Genocide of the Armenians and the Silence of the Turks" in *Problems of Genocide*.

[16] A. Hovanissian, "Turkey: A Cultural Genocide" in *Problems of Genocide*.

[17] Zoryan Institute, *The Armenian Experience: Profile* (Chicago, Zoryan, 1984)

[18] The percentage of Jewish losses during the Holocaust have been calculated at 85% for Poland and 81% for Germany. See H. Voght, "Life in the Third Reich" in R. Waite, ed., *Hitler and Nazi Germany* (Hinsdale, Dryden Pres, 1965) p. 75.

[19] The role of the state is a key part of Horowitz's definition of genocide. I. Horowtiz, *Taking Lives: Genocide and State Power* (New Brunswick, Transaction, 1980, 3rd edition).

[20] For example the following is a comprehensive list of the Toronto *Globe*'s published story headlines and editorials in 1915: "Armenians Massacred in Hundred Villages" (May 24); "Turks Slay 14,000 in One Massacre" (August 26); "Armenian Refugees Declare That 70,000 Armenians Have Been Massacred" (September 9); "Turk's Fall to End Campaign of Murder: Terrible Atrocities are Committed in the Near East" (September 16); "The Cup of Turkey's Iniquity Full" (*Globe* editorial, September 22); "Armenians Rescued From Pursuing Turks: French Cruisers Go to Help the Refugees" (September 23); "Terrible Tales Told of Turkish Massacres: Armenian Men Systematically Murdered -- Extermination the Watchword" (September 24); "Million Armenians Wiped Out by Turks: Only 200,000 Armenian Inhabitants of Turkey Now Remain in Country" (October 23); "No British Agents Fomenting Armenians: Massacres of Unsurpassing Horror Committed By Turks" (November 27); "Armenia: The Unspeakable Tragedy" (*Globe* editorial, December 2); "Million Armenians Massacred by Turks: Lord Bryce Publishes Further Report of Atrocities in Asia Minor" (December 15).

[21] See for example the statement in the House of Commons on February 15, 1999 by the NDP Member of Parliament Svend Robinson cited in L. Shirinian, *Quest for Closure*, p. 131.

[22] L. Shirinian, *Quest for Closure*, pp. 143-161.

[23] For many decades Germany was divided into two states (West and East Germany).

[24] M. Lippman, "Genocide" in M. Bassiouni, ed., *International Criminal Law*, Volume 1.

[25] Charles Humana, *World Human Rights Guide* (London, Pan, 1987, 1st edition, 1986 and N.Y., Oxford, 1992, 3rd edition).

[26] One does note, however, the efforts by Mustafa Kemal and the Young Turks to modernize the polity, but this is not necessarily the same as democratization. For a sympathetic account, see S. Shaw and E. Kural Shaw,

History of the Ottoman Empire and Modern Turkey Volume II, (Cambridge, Cambridge University Press, 1977).

[27] See for example D. Rustow, *Turkey: America's Forgotten Ally*, (N.Y., Council of Foreign Relations, 1989).

[28] Charles Humana, *World Human Rights Guide* (1st and 3rd editions). In comparison, Canada in the same period had an impressive domestic human rights score of 96% and 94% in 1986 and 1991.

[29] See L. *Quest For Closure*, #4, pp. 119-142.

[30] Amongst the traits of a civil society are a respect for individual and collective rights, equality of all, the power of the state is constrained in a constitutional manner, there exists a tolerant and pluralistic culture, and there is a respect by the majority for ethnic, religious and linguistic and other minorities. See S. DeLue, *Political Thinking, Political Theory and Civil Society* (Boston, Allyn and Bacon, 1997).

[31] For example, one notes that in 1928 Canada's Governor General Willingdon was the official patron on the Armenian Relief Association of Canada. See L. Shirinian, *Quest for Closure*, pp. 66, 119-120.

[32] See for example Jim Karygiannis, Sarkis Assadourian, Julian Reed, (Liberal) on the government side and Svend Robinson (NDP) and Daniel Turp (BQ) on the opposition side. L. Shirinian, *Quest for Closure*, pp. 129-131. On February 15, 1999, Karygiannis had introduced a private member's bill calling for the House of Commons to officially recognize the 1915 genocide.

[33] For example, note the Turkish Ambassador's July 12, 1999 letter to the *Globe and Mail*, and a subsequent follow-up letter to the *Globe* dated August 12, 1999 by the First Counsellor (not published). FAX copy provided to the author. See also comparable correspondence in the *Toronto Star*.

[34] Perhaps most notable internationally was the Near East Relief, while in Canada it was the Armenian Relief Association of Canada. See L. Shirinian, *Quest For Closure*.

[35] For details, see L. Shirinian, *Quest for Closure*, pp. 110, 131.

[36] See Svend Robinson's speech in the House of Commons, February 15, 1999 cited by L. Shirinian, *Quest for Closure*, p.131.

[37] See W. Stanbury, "Regulating Federal Party and Candidate Finances in a Dynamic Environment" in H. Thorburn and A. Whitehorn, eds., *Party Politics in Canada* (Toronto, Pearson Education, 2000, 8th edition).

[38] The Honourable Ed Broadbent, former Director of the Montreal-based International Centre for Human Rights and Democratic Development suggests this very point in his "Introduction" to L. Shirinian's *Quest for Closure* when he states: "Ignoring the evidence in their own files about Turkey's role, Liberal spokespersons are into official denial. Such action undermines in its inconsistency the serious arguments justifying military intervention in Kosovo." One notes with interest the recent appointment of Louise Arbour to the Supreme

Court of Canada following her work with the International Criminal Tribunal for the Former Yugoslavia in the Hague on war crimes relating to ethnic cleansing in the Balkans.

[39] E. Broadbent's "Introduction" to L. Shirinian's *Quest for Closure*.

[40] One notes similar reactions by war veteran military soldiers who inspected the Nazi death camps in WWII or witnessed part of the forced deportations and genocide of Armenians in 1915. See for example the comments of U.S. Major General James Harbord when he stated "Mutilation, violation, torture and death have left their haunting memories in a hundred beautiful Armenian valleys, and the traveler [sic] in that region is seldom free from the evidence of this most colossal crime of all the ages." *International Conciliation* CLI (N.Y., June 1920) reprinted in V. Dadrian, ed., *The Ottoman Empire: A Troubled Legacy*, p. 55. US Ambassador to Turkey Henry Morgenthau states in his memoirs: "From American consuls and missionaries I was constantly receiving reports of such executions, and many of the events which they described will never fade from my memory." and "Though all sorts of impediments were placed to travelling, certain Americans, chiefly missionaries, succeeded in getting through. For hours they would sit in my office and, with tears streaming down their faces, they would tell me of the horrors through which they had passed. Many of these, both men and women, were almost broken in health from the scenes which they had witnessed. In many cases they brought me letters from American consuls, confirming the most dreadful of their narrations and adding many unprintable details." H. Morgenthau, *Ambassador Morgenthau's Story* (Garden City, Doubleday, Page, 1919) pp. 311-312, 327-328.

[41] One notes the experience of Canadian UN peacekeepers in Rwanda and in particular the plight of General Dallaire whose traumatic reaction has led to his premature retirement from active service in the Canadian military. Sadly, his severe psychological shock and depression were comparable to a number of outside observers of the 1915 genocide.

[42] See for example J. Porter, ed., *Genocide and Human Rights: A Global Anthology* and National Association for Armenian Studies and Research, *Genocide and Human Rights: Lessons From the Armenian Experience* (Belmont, Armenian Heritage Press, 1993; special issue of the *Journal of Armenian Studies*).

[43] For a listing of the headlines, see an earlier footnote in this chapter.

[44] See for example V. Dadrian, ed., *The Ottoman Empire: A Troubled Legacy – Views, Comments and Judgments by Noted Experts Worldwide* (Association of Genocide Scholars, Zoryan, Cambridge, 1997) provides an important compendium of important archival quotes and sources on the subject.

[45] Press release of "Statement of the President" www.pub.whitehouse.gov/uri-res/I2R?urn:pdi//oma.eop.gov.us/1999/4/20/6.test,

April 19, 1999. See also L. Shirinian, *Quest for Closure*, p. 139.

[46] Indeed, the drafter of the United Nation's Universal Declaration of Human Rights (December 10, 1948) was a Canadian. John Humphrey (1905-1995), a former law professor at McGill University, also served for almost two decades as the first Head of the UN Division of Human Rights. See W. Kaplan, "John Peters Humphrey" in *The Canadian Encyclopedia* (McClelland and Stewart, Toronto, 1999). See also the Department of Canadian Heritage's 1998 web page devoted to the fiftieth anniversary of the Declaration. www.credo98.com/credo50/50udh.html.

[47] Even Hitler seemed to have recognized this linkage of one genocide with another. See K. Bardakjian, *Hitler and the Armenian Genocide* (Cambridge, Zoryan, 1985).

[48] The originator of the term genocide, Raphael Lemkin is said to have been profoundly influenced by the example of the Armenian case and the gap in international criminal law. See J. Tashjian, "Genocide, the United Nations and the Armenians, in J. Porter, ed., *Genocide and Human Rights: A Global Anthology*.

[49] This is powerfully conveyed in the Department of National Defence's 1998 documentary video entitled *Witness the Evil* where General Dallaire and other Canadian soldiers describe their suffering from "post-traumatic stress" following their UN tour of duty in Rwanda. In some ways it is remarkably similar to that of earlier accounts by witnesses of the 1915 genocide.

[50] M. Minow, *Between Vengeance and Forgiveness: Facing History after Genocide and Mass Violence* (Boston, Beacon, 1998). There seems to be a general sequence in dealing with genocide. For the first generation there is the trauma of the actual genocide and seeking bare physical survival. Later from a safer locale, there is either a preoccupation with punishment and/or revenge (e.g. assassinations in Europe of some of key figures) or recommencing as best possible a normal family life. For the second generation there may be the desire for some sort of assimilation into their new society, but there is also an attempt to intellectually understand the catastrophic events and recreate an identity in the Diaspora.

[51] J. Kogawa, "Foreword" in L. Shirinian, *Quest for Closure*.

[52] This is also a theme in Minow, *Between Vengeance and Forgiveness*, chapter #4 "Truth Commissions". See also A. Henkin, ed., *Honoring Human Rights From Peace to Justice* (Washington, Aspen Institute, 1999) p. 17.

[53] See "Turkish Region Recalls Massacre of Armenians", *New York Times*, May 10, 2000.

[54] The Reverend J.S. Woodsworth was one of the most famous Members of Parliament and the first leader of the national CCF. He was author of the pioneering book *Strangers Within Our Gates* about the plight of immigrants in our large cities.

The Armenian Genocide and Its Aftermath: Genocide Denial, a Canadian Perspective

Lorne Shirinian

The Armenian Genocide of 1915, one of the most blatant and heinous examples of human rights abuses, has been very well documented throughout the years from eyewitness reports, government documents and historical studies. Every year, new findings come to light that allow us to get an even clearer understanding of what occurred; for example, material from the German archives is now being researched and has yielded new information on that state's participation in the events along with its Ottoman ally. On April 24, 1915, the Ottoman Turkish government rounded up some 200 Armenian intellectuals and community leaders, took them from their homes, and killed them. This signaled what would become the pattern that was followed in the years that followed. In towns and villages throughout the Ottoman Empire, those Armenians who had not already been taken, were marched away where they were continually set upon by brigands, (*chetes*, set free from the prisons and jails for the express purpose of killing Armenians), raped or killed outright by the gendarmes who forced marched them away without food, water or clothing towards the deserts of Mesopotamia. Those who survived the march then faced starvation and disease. In all, between the years 1915 and 1923, perhaps 1.5 million Armenians who had lived in the Ottoman Empire were killed in this way. The Western Armenian homeland is now, for all intents and purposes, devoid of any significant Armenian population.

We know that the deadly effects of genocide do not end when the actual hostilities end as they did for the Armenians in 1923. Rather, they continue, particularly if there has been no resolution or chance for the victims to heal, throughout generations. Thus, Armenians find themselves in the first year of the new millennium, still searching for a resolution to the genocide, the catastrophe inflicted upon them in 1915.

This paper deals with memory, genocide denial, and the complicity of the Canadian government in the very act of this denial to the detriment of a community of its citizens. It may appear at first that we are a long way from Asia Minor, but the terrible human rights abuses began there 85 years ago still haunt the sons and daughters, grandsons and granddaughters of those who were fortunate to have survived. In this way, the genocide still continues.

On April 24th this year, Armenians gathered to commemorate the Armenian Genocide—the second such commemoration of the new millennium. Eighty-five years after the terrible events began in 1915, one notes that there are fewer and fewer survivors each year as the Turkish denial grows stronger and more persistent. For Armenians, memory and the imperative to remember are crucial acts. Memory is the knowledge of past events. An understanding of the past informs Armenians that the founding of their community, that is, the modern Armenian diaspora in North America, comes from acts of violence. One must guard against rendering the Armenian diaspora homogeneous; nevertheless, much of Armenian identity in the diaspora is based on violent events. In this way, part of their collective identity is a storehouse of violence, wounds, and scars. For Armenians, remembering, the act of exercising memory, has the potential to turn knowledge into action. This is the ethical-political component of memory as it refers to the construction of the future for the Armenian community. Consequently, the duty to remember means having a concern for the past and transmitting the meaning of these past events to future generations. Armenians know, perhaps more than most people, the necessity to speak of the Genocide, for to do so is to fight against the erosion of their traces in this world. The Turkish intention is to complete the destruction begun in 1915 through genocide denial. As history is most often written and legitimized by victors, it becomes a duty to remember and speak out. Communities are created and developed by the stories they recount to themselves and to others. To a certain extent, therefore, identity, memory, and narrative are inextricably linked. By speaking out, one gives voice to the victims.

Remembering and speaking out become a moral duty, and by doing so, one pays a debt to the victims of the Genocide. Furthermore, through memory and speaking out, one prevents forgetfulness from destroying the victims yet a second time.

Today, this has taken on a greater urgency than ever before because of the continued genocide denial of successive Turkish governments.

Genocide is a form of mass murder planned and executed by a state. In order to eliminate a national minority like the Armenians in Turkey, the government in power and its state institutions such as the army and the police must have been involved.[1] Given the continued genocide denial of the Turkish Republic to deflect blame, legal consequences, and external rebuke, a veritable propaganda industry of denial has been developed.[2] The relative success of the deniers depends on two factors. First, the process of denial takes advantage of our inherent sense of fair play and willingness to hear both sides of an issue, and secondly, denial requires no proof, only an assertion and a call for a re-evaluation of history. The onus, then, is placed on someone else—usually the victims—to disprove the assertion.[3]

State-funded organizations in Turkey publish books which misrepresent Armenian history. This attack has two overriding goals: i) to prove that Western Armenia has never been the homeland of the Armenians, and ii) that Turks never committed the Genocide. The goal of the deniers is to confuse matters by making it appear as if they are engaged in an authentic scholarly pursuit, which they are not.

The strategy of denial by the Turkish government has evolved over the years from outright negation to rationalization, relativization, and trivialization. As Richard Hovannisian has written,

> These forms of denial are intended to create doubts and cloak disinformation by appealing to a sense of fair play and of giving a hearing to the other side of a misunderstood and misrepresented issue. Prejudice and

stereotyping, the deniers maintain, are residues of historical scapegoating or wartime propaganda and the machinations of the alleged victims to enrich themselves personally and collectively at the expense of others.[4]

In an article titled "Rewriting History—Killing Truth" in the *Washington Post* (May 31, 1983), Richard Cohen wrote, "The last victim of any genocide is truth."[5] He wrote the article after hearing the Ambassador of Turkey explaining at the embassy that "there never was a policy to exterminate the Armenians."[6] In his article, Cohen concludes, "And so year by year, person by person, the genocide blurs, doubt corrodes it, and the easy word 'alleged' creeps in to mock the Armenian anguish."[7] Denial is the final phase of genocide. After the destruction of the people and the remnants of their material culture, the final target becomes memory itself. To complete genocide, the annihilation of a people, necessitates an assault on any recollection of them. "Falsification, deception, and half-truths reduce what was to what may have been or perhaps what was not at all."[8] Thus, history becomes rewritten and finally unwritten. As the past is adjusted then erased, a new present is created without any care for historical integrity. Little by little, the Genocide is taken further, another step closer to being completed until the last orphan of memory is buried.[9] This is what the Armenian people have been subjected to in their various host countries since 1915, and Canada is no exception.

A series of events in the late 1980s and 1990s gave some indication as to how the Armenian Genocide was pursued in certain sectors of Canadian society. The first of these events is the Ottawa Board of Education incident.[10]

In order to deal more effectively with the rapidly changing multicultural nature of Canadian society, the Ottawa Board of Education (OBE) on September 24, 1979, voted to constitute the Multiculturalism Advisory Committee (MAC) to study matters related to multiculturalism in the school system. One of the mandates of MAC was to provide background material to familiarize teachers and students with the history, traditions, values, and aspirations of the various cultural groups in the system. The desire was to assist students to retain their cultural identity by familiarizing them with the historical roots and culture of their communities and to develop in them a sense of continuity with their past, while at the same time helping them to learn and to appreciate the heritage of other Canadians.

The first contentious issue during MAC's deliberations concerning Armenians arose over the development of resource material on genocide. MAC suggested material on four case studies of genocide in the 20th century: the 1915 Armenian Genocide, the Baltic Genocide during the Stalinist era, the Jewish Holocaust Under the Nazis, and the Ukraine Forced Famine in the 1930s during Stalin's regime. Each of these tragedies provided a different example of genocide and was meant to give students an understanding of the two World Wars. The module came out in February 1988 and was titled "Man's Inhumanity to Man." The Armenian section is forty-two pages long, chronological in nature and begins with maps, a glossary, questions and complete references to sources. At the end, six pages are given over to the contrary Turkish view that no genocide took place; this was an omen of what was to follow in the subsequent draft.

It did not take long for outside political pressure to rise. In March 1988, the Department of External Affairs said that "the Ottawa board of education should respect the Turkish government's position that there was no Armenian genocide."[11] Jacques Roy, the assistant deputy minister of the department's Europe branch, objected to the inclusion of the subject in the new curriculum. In a two-page letter to the board chairperson, Marjorie Loughrey, he wrote,

> I wish to indicate the federal government's concern about the negative impact the adoption of the program as presently formulated would have on Canadian-Turkish relations.... On many occasions, the Turkish authorities have expressed their concerns to us. They fear that the use of the word genocide creates the association with Nazi and Soviet atrocities. They consider

that there is a bias against them in the selection of your study material and they believe this brings about a distorted impression of modern Turkey.[12]

Some school board trustees wondered whether the federal government had the right to question school curricula, particularly since education constitutionally is a provincial jurisdiction. The issue became explosive. Here was a case in which the federal government formally committed to the principles of multiculturalism and human rights actively lobbied against the dissemination of historical documents about the suffering of some of its own citizens. In so doing, the government engaged in genocide denial and turned its back on the extensive historical record. At a higher level, the Minister of External Affairs, Joe Clark, on March 18, 1988, apologized for the earlier departmental letter from his assistant deputy minister in which the Armenian Genocide was denied. In the House of Commons, Clark said that Roy's letter should not have been sent. "I understand the concern of the Canadian-Armenian community," he said. "I regret the letter was sent. It was a mistake. It is something that I deeply regret."[13] Roy, however, was recalcitrant. In an interview, he said that "Canada should accept Turkey's claim there was no genocide, in order not to jeopardize 'millions of dollars' in trade contracts."[14] Roy's attitude, unfortunately, has been too often typical of the way the Ministry of Foreign Affairs has considered Canadian Armenians and their quest to have the Genocide recognized. For the Canadian government, commercial contracts and pleasing foreign governments and corporations are more important than a moral stand and the historical record.

The issue did not end with Clark's apology, however. By 1990, major changes had occurred in the table of contents of the genocide material, which now reads as follows: Baltic Countries, The Holocaust, Japanese Canadians, Ottoman Turks/Armenians, Ukraine. In all but the Armenian case, genocide for the OBE was clear. However, the curriculum now indicated that there were two versions in the Armenian case and that a counterbalancing of views was necessary. The implication was that the OBE was inviting its teachers and students to consider that perhaps there never was an Armenian genocide. This skeptical and comparative approach in which contrasting views on the same issue are presented was not applied to any of the other cases. No Neo-Nazi position was offered on the Holocaust, for example, as abhorrent a thought as that may be. Board members had clearly changed their views on the subject. Commercial considerations prevailed over morality.

The second incident in which the Turkish government and lobby attempted to eliminate any reference to the Armenian Genocide in Canada took place in Montreal in 1997-1998 and was focused around the desire of the Armenian community there to erect a monument to those who were killed during the Genocide.

In 1994, Montreal Mayor, Pierre Bourque, promised the construction of a monument honouring the victims of the 1915 Genocide. Seventy-five thousand dollars was budgeted to lay a foundation at Marcelin-Wilson Park in the north end of the city; to this, the Armenian community added $100,000. However, Bourque later shelved the plans after being pressured by the federal government and the Turkish community.[15] As well, five Quebec companies, Pyrox Technologies, Inc., Tecksol, Mabarex, Napco Housing, Inc., and Walsh Automation, eager to do business with Turkey, demanded that Mayor Bourque not build the monument, complaining in letters that they could lose lucrative contracts if the city went ahead with its plans. The Turkish government also pressured Bourque by threatening to cancel a visit by its environment minister and a business delegation. Florian Bessette, vice-president of Napco Housing, which had just signed a multimillion-dollar deal with the Istanbul Chamber of Commerce to build 10,000 prefabricated housing units in Turkey, said in her letter to Bourque, "We firmly believe that if you go ahead with this project, it will jeopardize all our efforts at commercial cooperation with Turkey."[16] Federal cabinet minister, Pierre Pettigrew admitted telling Bourque about his government's position on the Genocide, but denied putting pressure on the mayor. Aaron Derfel, writing in *The Gazette* (Montreal), reminded his readers that Ottawa does not wish to offend Turkey, which has become a growing market for Canadian goods and services. In 1996, Canada exported $225 million worth of products to Turkey, almost doubling the total amount of business done there since 1992. Derfel went on to write that Turkey has insisted that a state-sponsored genocide never existed, but told his readers that,

> Evidence exists, however, that up to 1.5 million Armenians were killed in the genocide. In their authoritative book, *The History and Sociology of Genocide*, Concordia University professors Frank Chalk and Kurt Jonassohn corroborate the Armenians' case.[17]

In the end, Bourque decided to go ahead with the building of the monument but not without initially refusing to include any reference to the number of people who perished. However, needing to reconcile with the local Armenian community before the next municipal election one year away, he reversed his decision once again, and the monument was unveiled with reference to the numbers killed during the Genocide Commemoration in Montreal on April 26, 1998.

These two incidents are typical of the obstacles Canadian Armenians must overcome, not only by the intransigent Turkish government and its lobby, but also by its own government, to gain recognition of the Genocide.

In March 1999, the Minister of Foreign Affairs, Lloyd Axworthy, convened a Liberal party committee to study the Armenian Genocide issue and to make a recommendation to him by April 13, 1999. The Zoryan Institute in Toronto was requested to prepare a background paper for the committee as it is the primary academic and scholarly body in this country that has for one of its principal areas of inquiry, the Armenian Genocide. As this author participated in the writing of this report, along with several colleagues, I am aware of the process and the government's response. It may be instructive to go through a brief history of how and why this question arose at this time.

On Monday, February 15, 1999, Jim Karygiannis, the Liberal MP for Scarborough-Agincourt, brought a motion to the House of Commons as private members' business. He asked that the House:

> (a) join the members of the Armenian Canadian community in honouring the memory of the 1.5 million men, women, and children who fell victim of the first genocide of the 20th century;
> (b) condemn the genocide of the Armenians and all other acts of genocide committed during our century as the ultimate act of racial, religious and cultural intolerance;
> (c) recognize the importance of remembering and learning from such dark chapters in human history to ensure that such crimes against humanity are not allowed to be repeated;
> (d) condemn and prevent all attempts to use the passage of time to deny or distort the historical truth of the genocide of the Armenians and other acts of genocide committed during this century;
> (e) designate April 24 of every year hereafter throughout Canada as a day of remembrance of the 1.5 million Armenians who fell victim to the first genocide of this century; and
> (f) call on the Government of Canada officially to condemn the genocide of the Armenians and any attempts to deny such crimes against humanity.[18]

The issue was now placed directly before the House of Commons; however, the history of success of private members' bills is not encouraging.

Julian Reed, the Parliamentary Secretary to the Minister of Foreign Affairs, was the first respondent to the motion made by MP Jim Karygiannis. He made what can only be called a speech written by those who would rewrite history and deny the Genocide. What is disconcerting is that the speech was written by officials in the Ministry of Foreign Affairs and betrays a systemic revisionist attitude that contradicts the government's official policy passed on April 23, 1996.

> That this House recognize, on the occasion of the 81st anniversary of the *Armenian Tragedy* (author's italics) which claimed some 1.5 million lives that took place on April 24, 1915, and in recognition of other crimes against humanity, the week of April 20 to 27 of each year as the week of remembrance of the inhumanity of people toward one another.

To add insult to injury, Reed said that "the Turkish people [are] profoundly hurt by the accusation of genocide."

Reed's speech uses the familiar techniques employed by the genocide deniers. His parliamentary speech suggested that, "there was enormous suffering for all the people involved in the 1915 events and that in addition to the death of soldiers there were literally millions of innocent civilian victims in this conflict on both sides." Here Reed makes use of a trick of the numbers game in order to relativize the Genocide and bury its effects within the conflict among the belligerents in World War I. It is like counting the number of Jews slaughtered with the number of dead Nazi soldiers in WWII. Reed mixes two distinct categories of losses into a single undifferentiated one. This allows him to produce misleading sums. First, there are the victims of state-sponsored mass murder. These civilians—adults and children alike—should be differentiated from those who died in battle with other armies or from war-related causes such as poor medical facilities. The report of American Major General Harbord in 1920 stated that, "Not over 20 percent of the Turkish peasants who went to war have returned…. Six hundred thousand Turkish soldiers died of typhus alone…and insufficient hospital service and absolute poverty of supply swelled the death lists." [19] In contrast to these victims were the conditions of the Armenian victims, which Harbord related as "the wholesale attempt on the [Armenian] race." He underscored the "evidence of this most colossal crime of all ages [involving] mutilation, violation, torture and death… Testimony is universal that the massacres have always been ordered from [the capital in] Constantinople." Official reports, according to Harbord showed 1,100,000 as having been deported. Harbord placed the number of Armenian victims of genocide at about 800,000.

Reed made use of yet another argument that deniers use which is the question of Armenian self-defence that took place in several towns in the eastern provinces such as Van. He suggested that, "young Armenian males should have been conscripted into the army along with Muslims, but tens of thousands escaped to join guerilla bands or fled to Russia.... The general picture that is created is that of a rebellious Armenian population which had particular affinities with the Russian invading army, one of them being the Christian religion." Presumably, the purpose of this kind of argument is to create the idea that there was a civil war that resulted from weakened authority from the central government. The implication is that Armenians engaged in armed conflict with Turkish soldiers. By such perverse logic, the Warsaw uprising of Jews would then justify the Holocaust of six million Jews. However, as one looks at the facts of this argument, one sees that it defies logic. First of all, on August 3, 1914, a full three months before Turkey even began the war with Russia, all able-bodied men, including those of Armenian heritage, between the ages of 20 and 45, then later between 18 and 20, and finally, as the government became even more desperate, those between 45 and 60 were conscripted into the Ottoman army. Not long after, most of the Armenian conscripts were separated out by government decree and massacred. Those that were left in Armenian towns and villages were mostly old men, women and children, who still recalled the massacres of their people in the 1895-96 pogroms. By the summer of 1915, most of these villagers had been deported, and if they were lucky to have survived at all, were starving and emaciated. A genocide cannot be disguised as a major civil war, even eight decades later. To make such an implication is historically inaccurate and morally repugnant.

As was the case of the Warsaw uprising in World War II, there were several isolated and disconnected incidents of resistance to the Genocide as the ethnic cleansing and mass deportations became known. For example, some 500-600

Armenians in Van aided by about 1,000 support people rose up to prevent the Turks from deporting and destroying the Armenian population of the city and the surrounding area. Turkish forces attempted to encircle the town and to reduce and overrun it but failed to overwhelm the defenders. The Turkish divisions suffered heavy losses and fled Van as Russian troops were advancing rapidly from the east. The Armenians of Van held off the Turkish soldiers from April 20 to May 17, 1915. Vice Marshal Pomiankowski of Austria, who was attached to the Ottoman General Headquarters described the uprising as an act of desperation to avert a general slaughter. Rafael de Nogales, a Venezuelan artillery officer with the Ottoman army, reports that Turkish authorities had initiated the attack on the Armenians of Van; "he [the Turkish military commander at Van] was doing nothing more than carrying out an unequivocal order emanating from the governor of the province...to exterminate all Armenian males of twelve years of age and over."[20] De Nogales' testimony is important because, as he states it, he was "the only Christian who witnessed the Armenian massacres and the deportations in an official capacity...."[21]

Mr. Reed refers to the mass deportations and slaughter of the Armenian population as "relocation," a term which, in light of the well-documented history, is shameful. Reed stated, "They [Armenians] perished mainly due to disease, harsh weather, exposure and hunger. This is the episode that many Armenians believe constitutes genocide. They portray this deportation as a decision aimed at exterminating the Armenian population in general." Without referring to the numerous survivor memoirs in which one finds detailed descriptions of what *relocation*—the Turkish government's euphemism for mass deportation and slaughter—meant, there is enough evidence for us to understand its real intent. The legal councilor at the German embassy in Istanbul, Dr. Otto Göppert characterized *relocation*, as a farce when he reported it to Berlin.[22] The Special Agent of the State Department, Lewis Epstein, who was on duty at the American Embassy in Istanbul during the Genocide period described what *relocation* would mean.

> New homes would be provided for them, [the deportees], at Zor and in the desert land, through which flows the Euphrates. Such was the official euphemism...the grim humor of paternal solicitude which usually covers the most barbarous massacres in Turkey.... [What was involved here was] an armed policy of deportation, and its implied sequel, extermination.... The diabolical plot aimed at making the Armenians run the whole gauntlet of Asia Minor, where the country had been aroused to murder.[23]

Vice Marshal Pomiankowski in his memoirs wrote that "the barbaric order to deport and resettle in the northern desert region of Arabia, i.e. Mesopotamia...the entire Armenian population of Asia Minor in reality entailed the extermination of Asia Minor's Armenian population.[24] A Turkish intelligence officer at Department II, Ottoman General Headquarters, Ahmet Refik (Altinay), stated that those deportees who were fortunate to escape massacre "were driven to blazing deserts, to hunger, misery and death."[25] Finally, the Turkish historian, Taner Akçam, offers a similar observation on the fate of relocated Armenians,

> The fact that neither at the start of the deportations, nor en route, and nor at the locations, which were declared to be their initial halting places, were there any... arrangements, required for the organization of a people's migration, is sufficient proof of the existence of this plan of annihilation.[26]

As one reads the evidence, the wall of denial is easily dismantled, lie by lie, distortion by distortion. That a Canadian parliamentarian should make use of such arguments on an issue of such importance as genocide is damning.

Sarkis Assadourian, the Liberal MP from Brampton Centre, expressed shock at the speech made by the Parliamentary

Secretary for the Minister of Foreign Affairs, and that a member of his own government could bring such material and represent the government's position in that way. The general outcry from the Armenian population in Canada when word of Mr. Reed's speech was made known prompted the Honorable Lloyd Axworthy to say in the House of Commons on February 17th the following:

> Mr. Speaker, it is very important that Canadians recognize the serious tragedy experienced by the Armenian people. To further that I have asked the Canadian Armenian community to meet with me so that we can foster a broad dialogue that will help develop understanding, heal wounds and forward the process of reconciliation among all Canadians about this very serious tragedy that occurred many years ago.

In an attempt to heal wounds this speech had created in the Armenian community, Minister Axworthy set up a government committee chaired by Derek Lee, Liberal MP for Scarborough-Rouge River, to study the question and to present a report to him as to whether or not the government should officially recognize the Armenian Genocide. As mentioned above, the Zoryan Institute of Canada, because of its reputation of scholarship and objectivity, was asked verbally by Mr. Lee to write a background report for his committee to consider. The instructions were to focus on the way the events of the Armenian Genocide can be considered a genocide, according to the definition adopted by the United Nations. In a telephone call placed by Zoryan's chairperson, Professor Varouj Aivazian, to Derek Lee during the following week, he was told by Mr. Lee's secretary that he [Derek Lee] would be having a meeting with two Turkish professors that afternoon. Soon after, Lee sent the Zoryan Institute a letter asking for a report; however, now the instructions had changed. In his letter dated March 16, 1999, Mr. Lee asked the Institute for a three-page "'backgrounder' to assist me and my colleagues in discussion of issues arising from the House of Commons debate of Private Member's Motion M-329 on February 15, 1999." The Institute was now faced with reducing the events of the Armenian Genocide to three pages. However, the format he proposed presented even more problems. Below are the questions he asked the Institute to consider.

1. Where (geographic location) and When (over what time period) were Armenians (linguistically/culturally/religiously) brought into conflict with government forces or other "people" within the Ottoman Empire (in or near present-day Turkey) in the period during and following the First World War?
2. What were the kinds of acts of force/violence/cruelty directed at those who were (linguistically/culturally/ religiously) Armenian?
3. Is there a need to describe the political or economic context which existed in the region at the time? If yes, what was it?
4. Were there other countries exerting a materially relevant influence on these events? If so, which and how?
5. Did the government of the region, or other governments, formally or otherwise, articulate any policy rationale for their role(s), if any, in these events? If so, please provide a reference.

The members of the Zoryan committee felt the questions seemed designed to deflect the issue of genocide and to place and to limit the events within the context of World War I. Consequently, the Institute decided to get yet another scholar's opinion, and to this end, it contacted Dr. Roger Smith, Professor of Government at the College of William and Mary, in Williamsburg, Virginia. Professor Smith is the President of the Association of Genocide Scholars and is an expert in the field of genocide and genocide denial. Below, is a portion of his response.

An advantage of those who wish to deny the Armenian Genocide is that they don't have to prove anything, only create doubt. While the five questions submitted by Derek Lee may seem reasonable, they favor the deniers, who can in a few words claim that the events were not a genocide, but a civil war, or the result not of any state intention, but of wartime conditions, which claimed the lives of both Turks and Armenians. Questions 3-5 play into the hands of the deniers—these questions are relevant but one cannot provide the context and substance in the three pages allowed. The first two questions seem better, although in 1, there is that strange language "brought into conflict with government forces...." This plays on the provocation thesis, and of Armenian rebellion.

On the other hand, if the questions did stick to the UN Convention on the Prevention and Punishment of Genocide, then it would be possible to address briefly the various genocidal acts that did take place (direct killing, placing people in situations calculated to lead to their death, transfer of children from one group to another, etc.) and to indicate some of the evidence of intent (a crucial element in genocide). On the latter, I did provide evidence of that (again briefly) in my article on "Professional Ethics and the Denial of the Armenian Genocide."[27]

The Zoryan Institute submitted its report to the government committee, which met on April 13 and reacted favourably to it. Sources say that the committee recommended that Minister Axworthy use the word, *genocide*, and that Daniel Laprès, a foreign affairs policy advisor, worked with the Minister to bring a bill to the floor of the House in which it would be stated that the Armenian massacres conform to the UN definition of genocide. However, it appears that at the last minute the Prime Minister's Office (PMO) interfered as civil servants in the Ministry of Foreign Affairs informed the PMO what was going to happen. The caucus committee never knew what was taking place behind the scene. In the end, the bill never appeared. In the House of Commons on June 6, 1999, Sarkis Assadourian (Brampton Centre, Lib) asked: "Mr. Speaker, in February, in answer to my question in the House on the Armenian issue, the Minister of Foreign Affairs indicated that they had held a consultation process which involved members of parliament, concerned Canadian communities, historians and others. Could the Minister of Foreign Affairs please inform the House of any conclusions that have been reached as a result of the consultation?"[28]

As Minister Axworthy was not in the House that day, his Parliamentary Secretary, Julian Reed, read the government's official response.

> Mr. Speaker, I thank the hon. member and all those who worked on this process. On behalf of the Minister of Foreign Affairs I wish to inform the House that together with all Canadians we remember the calamity afflicted on the Armenian people in 1915. This tragedy was committed with the intent to destroy a national group in which hundreds of thousands of Armenians were subject to atrocities which included massive deportations and massacres.
>
> May the memory of this period contribute to healing wounds as well as to the reconciliation of present day nations and communities and remind us all of our collective duty to work together toward world peace.[29]

The intent of the wording is clear; however, the statement does not include the essential word, *genocide*. Once again, the Canadian government missed another opportunity to take the moral high ground and use the word, *genocide*. Sadly, it was not done. One can speculate that the Prime Minister's desire to sell a

CANDU reactor to Turkey took precedence over the human rights of a community of Canadian citizens.

Finally, one recent example of the way the denial of the Armenian Genocide in Canada is still active is illustrative. It is subtle, but nonetheless pernicious in its attempt. In *The Toronto Star*, Sunday, July 4, 1999, Harry Sterling, a retired Canadian diplomat who had been posted in Turkey wrote an opinion piece titled "Freedom fighters, or terrorists?" The piece begins with comments on the Kurdistan Workers Party (PKK) and Abdullah Oçalan receiving the death penalty then goes on to various groups and states which have used terror for political ends such as the IRA and the PLO, Libya and Iraq. The seventh paragraph of the article focuses on Armenians.

> Unfortunately, seemingly just causes can be subverted by unpardonable acts of brutality, even barbarism, taken in revenge for perceived historical grievances and past wrongs. To this day, Armenians regularly try to assassinate Turkish diplomats—as they did twice in Canada's own capital, Ottawa—in revenge for alleged genocide committed against Armenians in Turkey during World War I.[30]

In the context of Sterling's article and the tone throughout, the entire piece is full of the rhetoric of genocide denial and historical revisionism. Sterling calls the recognition of the Armenian Genocide a "seemingly just cause." The author's implication, of course, is that it is not a just cause and even that there is no cause at all. He then goes on to call acts committed by a handful of Armenian terrorists "unpardonable acts of brutality, even barbarism" without raising in explanation the issue of the Genocide and the 1.5 million who were brutally massacred in acts of unimaginable barbarism. He adds disinformation to his piece by stating that "To this day, Armenians regularly try to assassinate Turkish diplomats." This is false. No Armenian terrorist activities have taken place since the late 1980s. The implication is that Armenians are still carrying out their past campaign of terrorist violence. Sterling continues, calling the Genocide "perceived historical grievances and past wrongs," again implying that they really do not exist in fact. He is thus able to dismiss the historical record of the Armenian Genocide finally by calling it "alleged." One can see how those who would deny the Genocide couch their language in phrases that "seemingly" might be true. To this, they add falsehoods and misinformation to further obfuscate the historical record, and those who are not aware of the history are prone to doubt the record or even to believe the attempts to rewrite history. I responded and *The Toronto Star* printed my letter.[31]

    These are the continual struggles Armenians have had to wage in countries around the world against the power of the Turkish state's denial of the Genocide. Sadly, not only must Armenians be alert to the various forms of denial and revisionism from Turkey, but they must also be on guard against the way their fellow citizens and their own governments, often in search of commerce, react to this. Needless to say, corporations and governments want trade and exports and too often are willing to turn a blind eye to grave injustice in the search for another sale.

    Despite the moral lapses of others, there have been some Turkish scholars in Europe and even some brave publishers in Turkey such as Dr. Ragip Zarakolu, who have looked at the Armenian Genocide openly and are beginning to understand the effects of genocide denial on their own country. Another such courageous scholar, Taner Akçam, an independent researcher in Hamburg, Germany, writes that it is incumbent on Turks to remember the Genocide that was treated in Turkish history as a non-event and denied so that "we [Turks] may 'recover it in our consciousness' and to assign to it the proper significance....A start can only be made by way of discovering the meaning of belonging to the perpetrator group and of bearing collective responsibility....I am of the opinion that the formation of the Turkish national identity played a decisive role not only in the decision to commit genocide but also in the current denial and tabooing of it."[32] His book, *Human Rights and the Armenian Question* (English translation), based in part on this subject, has been published in Turkey but cannot be reviewed. One wants to be hopeful that a dialogue among some members of this new generation of Turkish scholars and Armenian scholars can continue to develop.

The Armenian Genocide is, in the end, a problem for all humanity. Israel Charny reminds us that "We must fight denial of past genocides, not only to set the record of the past straight, but to fight evil in our time, relentlessly, courageously, and toughly."[33] The denial of any people's genocide is an affront to us all. We know the results of forgetting, as the relationship of the Armenian Genocide to the Holocaust has been well understood, not only by scholars after the fact, but especially by Hitler, who asked his military commanders in a speech during a planning session on August 22, 1939, for the invasion of Poland, "Who, after all, speaks today of the annihilation of the Armenians?"[34] One Israeli scholar has even called the Armenian Genocide the "dress rehearsal" for the Holocaust.[35] The Canadian government's recognition of the facts would be a major step towards righting a great wrong and helping to affirm that "the struggle of man against power is the struggle of memory against forgetting,"[36] as the Czech novelist, Milan Kundera, has written. Armenians will never forget the Genocide of their people. They ask that the Canadian government not continue to side with those who would deny the historical record and in good conscience recognize the Genocide that has so greatly affected the lives of a community of its citizens. In this way, Canada can become a moral beacon for other countries, a role it has aspired to for many decades.

[1] Yves Ternon, "The State's Crime: On the Subject of the Armenian and the Jewish Genocides," *Genocide and Human Rights: Lessons from the Armenian Experience.* A Special Issue of the *Journal of Armenian Studies* 4.1-2 (1992): 97.

[2] Vahakn Dadrian, *The Key Elements in the Turkish Denial of the Armenian Genocide: A Case Study of Distortion and Falsification* (Toronto and Cambridge, MA.: The Zoryan Institute, 1999) 1.

[3] Dadrian, *Key Elements...*, 1-2.

[4] Richard G. Hovannisian, "Denial of the Armenian Genocide in Comparison with Holocaust Denial," *Rembrance and Denial: The Case of the Armenian Genocide*, Richard G. Hovannisian, editor (Detroit: Wayne State University Press, 1998) 201.

[5] Quoted in Israel Charny, "A Contribution to the Psychology of Denial of Genocide," *Genocide and Human Rights: Lessons from the Armenian Experience.* A Special Issue of the *Journal of Armenian Studies* 4.1-2 (1992): 289.

[6] Quoted in Charny 289.

[7] Quoted in Charny 289.

[8] Hovannisian 202.

[9] Hovannisian 202.

[10] The information that follows in this section has been developed from the official minutes of the meetings, memos, and official documents of the Multicultural Advisory Committee of the Ottawa Board of Education. They were given to me by Garbis Armen, who represented the Armenian community on the advisory committee. I am grateful to him for sharing his first-hand knowledge of the events.

[11] "Genocide course upsets the Turks," *Vancouver Sun* (March 17, 1988) A6.

[12] "Genocide course upsets the Turks," *Vancouver Sun* (March 17, 1988) A6.

[13] "Clark sorry for letter denying 1915 genocide," *The Gazette* (Friday, March 18, 1988) B16.

[14] "Clark sorry for letter denying 1915 genocide," *The Gazette* (Friday, March 18, 1988) B16.

[15] "Armenian holocaust memorial okayed," *The Gazette* (Friday, October 24, 1997) A3.

[16] "Don't build Armenian monument, mayor told," *The Gazette* (October 29, 1997) A3.

[17] "Don't build Armenian monument, mayor told," *The Gazette* (October 29, 1997) A3.

[18] From the Federal Government's web site: http://www.parl.gc.ca/36/1/parlbus/chambus...e/debates/181_1999-02-15/han181_1100-e.htm

[19] Harbord Report to the U. S. Secretary of State, "American Military Mission to Armenian." International Conciliation CLI (151) New York, (June 1920) 280, 281, 282. Cited in Vahakn N. Dadrian, *Key Elements in the Denial of the Armenian Genocide: A Case Study of Distortion and Falsification* (The Zoryan Institute: Toronto and Cambridge, MA: 1999) 26.

[20] De Nogales and Pomiankowski cited in Vahakn N. Dadrian, *Warrant for Genocide: Key Elements of Turko-Armenian Conflict* (New Burnswick, NJ: Transaction Publishers, 1999) 116-117. The information on Van comes from Dadrian, pp 116-117.

[21] Rafael de Nogales, *Four Years Beneath the Crescent*, translated by M. Lee, (New York: Scribner's, 1926) 1, 72-97.

[22] Cited in Vahakn N. Dadrian, *The History of the Armenian Genocide: Ethnic Cleansing from the Balkans to Anatolia to the Caucasus* Providence and Oxford: Berghahn Books, 1995) 241.

[23] Cited in Dadrian, *The History of the Armenian Genocide...*, 241.

[24] Cited in Dadrian, *The History of the Armenian Genocide...*, 242.

[25] Cited in Dadrian, *The History of the Armenian Genocide...*, 243.

[26] Cited in Dadrian, *The History of the Armenian Genocide...*, 243.

[27] See Roger Smith, Erik Markusen, and Robert J. Lifton, "Professional Ethics and the Denial of the Armenian Genocide," in *Remembrance and Denial: The Case of the Armenian Genocide*, edited by Richard Hovannisian (Detroit: Wayne State University Press, 1999) 271-295.

[28] http://www.parl.gc.ca/36/1/parlbus/cham...ebates/242_1999-06-10/han242_1440-e.htm

[29] http://www.parl.gc.ca/36/1/parlbus/cham...ebates/242_1999-06-10/han242_1440-e.htm

[30] "Freedom fighters, or terrorists?" *The Toronto Star* (Sunday, July 4, 1999) A13.

[31] "Armenian genocide isn't just an allegation," *The Toronto Star* (Thursday, July 15, 1999) A23.

[32] Akçam 350-351.

[33] Charny 301.

[34] Quoted in Kevork Bardakjian, *Hitler and the Armenian Genocide* (Cambridge and Toronto: The Zoryan Institute, 1985) 1.
[35] Quoted in Charny 303. See note 15.
[36] Terrence Des Pres, "Introduction: Remembering Armenia," in *The Armenian Genocide in Perspective*, Richard Hovannisian, editor (New Brunswick, NJ: Transaction Books, 1986) 10.

Poems by Lorne Shirinian

From *Earthquake* (1991)

The Armenian Steps into the Postmodern

1
Who are we now?

the Armenian wonders
the Armenian is a question

the Armenian
              is
not daring
              much
more

how is he to know
snapped
like a dry wishbone

the Armenian wanders
through the dislocated
comfort

how is he to understand
how is he to

the Armenian is
        ambiguous
among the indeterminacies

2

    unable to recover
    the
            whole
  of   himself
          insecure
       between the pieces
                         the
  Armenian hides from history

  he prefers to live
                  metonymically
  trusting montages
                  one step removed
  he looks askew
                  at his life
  from its borders

the Armenian has learned the lies
language whispers to men
no longer does he
ask for meaning

6

a nightingale sings
the Armenian listens
the nightingale reminds him
of a page

the nightingale sings of a poem
bursting with ripe apples
the Armenian sees breasts

the nightingale sings of firm round breasts
the apples taste of desire
the nightingale sings
of the Armenian's desire

the Armenian asks
the nightingale
                       singing in a silent tree
sing to me of my desire
sing to me in my absence

the Armenian dreams of a nightingale
hears its song
feels the desire
unsure
and elusive
heavy with excess

the certainty of longing

From *Earthquake*

III

the swirling sun brought the news
columns driven south
columns driven east
the whirling of sabres and flesh
smoke and fire
pushing the acrid soot of our past
round in tumbling eddies
the gravity of our history
out and beyond Armenia(n)

where all ends and all begins

our words have lost their native language
the diaspora is a haven
for this land of tyrants and exile is so unreal
tinted postcards of a blurred mythology
fragments of bad archaeology
speak to your heart in a foreign tongue
> *you watch your father*
> *bury his head his hands*
> *as he tries to remember his family*
> *nightmare tremors*
> *in his damaged memory*
> *in Toronto*
> *awaiting a homecoming*

From *Rough Landing* (2000)

Evolution

(On looking at a photograph taken in Western Armenia
in 1915 and one taken of me in 1997)

look how my skin colour has changed
the light of my flesh is somewhat duller now
but my hair is clean and neat
combed just so
and note the clothes
though last year's cut
still freshly pressed
the whole presents a sense of inattentive style
a portrait of studied carelessness
do you see the book in hand
held with serious intent before the Massey Library

and you
lost brother from the lost homeland
standing incredulous before the foreigner's lens
having just come from the morning's labour in the fields
you are dressed in soiled cloth
and stand proud before your home
a loose arrangement of earth and stone

but why is your head raised in the air
do you call to your son only half seen beyond the frame
is it to signal
to warn of their certain arrival
do you point to the cloud of dust rising
like a threat over the western hills
is that fear in your eyes

when i place our pictures side by side
we stare at each other
and though 82 years have passed
since that day you stared apprehensively
at the camera
i understand your wonder
in my eyes i see what you felt that day
for i too look for signals beyond the city walls

i keep one bag packed
and on some dark moonless nights
i leave the car running
the map open
and bury a few gold coins under the flowers
by the front porch

Bones

Yarn of a cargo of Human Bones
Copyright, 1925, by the New York Times Company
    Special Cable to the New York Times

PARIS, Dec. 22, Marseilles is excited by a weird story of the arrival in that port of a ship flying the British flag and named the *Zan* carrying a mysterious cargo of 400 tons of human bones consigned to manufacturers there. The bones are said to have been loaded at Mudania on the Sea of Marmara and to be the remains of the victims of massacres in Asia Minor. In view of the rumours circulating it is expected that an inquiry will be instigated.

                From the *New York Times*, Tuesday, December 23,
                1924.

no one remembers like Armenians
not many have a deeper history
but ours is portable
carried as cargo from the bloody interior of Asia Minor
held captive in a dank hold
away from the dead homeland
culture as brittle as bone

for you Armenian history is soft and scented
a sweet fragrant soap for the boudoirs and salons of Europe
inhale deeply
partake of our ancient history
in a moment's breath
we will be imprinted in your mind's memory

bones and sweet soap
bones and delicate buttons carved from a child's rib
Armenian artefacts from the interior of Turkey

we have a deeper history
and no one remembers like Armenians

Poems by Alan Whitehorn

Ancestral Voices

One:

One historic year.
One cataclysmic event.
One unforgettable bleak memory.
One ominous political concept.
One people almost annihilated.
One blood-stained colour.

One orphan child,
and then another,
and another,...

Somehow, a nation survives.
One extended family grows.
One searing memory penetrates to the bone.
One horrific deed now a people's defining identity.
One people unable and unwilling to forget.
One terrible deed,
and endless nightmares it did beget.
We do not forget that one historic year.
One catastrophic event that defines who I am,
and who I always will be.
Now and forever.

Blood Red Poppies:

As far as my eye can see,
the blood red poppies appear like a vast sea.

The tempest now mostly passed,
in the gentle breeze the petals do move to and fro.
Tis as if each soul still has life, I somehow know.
The storm descended ever so fast.
Now the fields are mostly silent at last.

Black, bleak memories of so many innocent dead,
I live with the continuing nightmare – tis an awful dread.
Blood red poppies seem like an endless sea;
they seem to span an eternity.

Lament for A Nation – Armenia:

How is it possible that two generations later
acts of violence occur
seeking retribution for a seven decade old genocide?
In so doing,
those unborn in 1915 kill others also unborn seventy years past.
Seemingly, an incident so long ago.
Forgotten by virtually all.
Most needing atlases to discover where Armenia is or was.

Tragically for some the cries of one million or more dead souls
is a deadly chorus
that drives them into acts of vengeful desperation.

It began decades ago.
In the midst of war, devastation and mournful cries.
Why us? Help us. Save my child. I beg you.
Please God, at least the children.
And so, a few children were saved.

Saved, but not unaffected.
Lonely, insecure, terrified children,
thousands of orphans,
children of the darkness and the dread,
helpless refugees scattered, here and there,
without family and past friends.

Time passed.
These troubled children aged.
A scarred generation -- they grew.
As adults, they taught what they knew.
Death, insecurity and solitude.
So that a new generation arose,
confused.
Loneliness, insecurity, emptiness.

Without a family tree,
too painful to discuss
names lost in far off wastelands.
Thus, no history, no past emerged
to give continuity.

And so, I aged.
I am unable to fire a gun.
I will not provide funds.
I cannot hide a fugitive.
I shall not defend such recent terrorist deeds.
Yet, I understand.
I understand and weep.

Armenia, my beloved country
that I never knew.
What might have been,
but for the acts of a few.
So long ago...

So long ago, they say, that few remember to this day.
So long ago...
Armenia,
is it death or sleep?
I do not know.

Metzmama:

During World War I,
a young child, my grandmother,
saw her entire family rounded up and massacred.
She survived, but barely,
saved by the dedication and care of a few from afar.
For several years, that seemed an eternity,
this youngster inhabited an overcrowded, refugee camp.

Eighty years later,
I still feel the incredible pain,
and hear the deadly chorus's refrain:

Never forget.
Remember our maimed and dead in ditches lain.
Remember the frightened, orphaned children.
Never should we follow this evil path again.

Remember.
Remember and learn.
Remember and live.
Remember and forgive.
Remember and love.

* with special thanks to Joy, Nora and Juan.

Siroun's Lament:

In a remote Anatolian field somewhere that I do not know;
upon unmarked graves of the dead, I hope flowers do grow.

In the beginning, only suffering and endless tears were sown,
but as decades passed, love and understanding have also grown.

From one small child standing helpless and ever so frail,
and, despite a nation refusing to admit the ghastly tale,

a family somehow has been nurtured with love and respect,
and within the diaspora, a better life has come to expect.

We are children and grandchildren of the genocide,
but are now citizens of the world, we do decide.

We cannot ignore other peoples' suffering and pain,
whether amidst a remote desert or tropical rain.

The children of the genocide do live;
most recover, and some even forgive.

But we shall never forget
the torment that was beget

in the arid, Anatolian plain
where the tears turned to rain.

Remembering Together:

an afternoon of remembering
through the written and spoken word,
and through the pain of others,
together we share;
we hug and cry,
we live and die,
and we remember as best we can
of the inhumanity to our fellow man.

How Do We Remember the Dead?

How do we remember the so many dead?
How do we cope, if at all, with the awful dread?

Do we deny the existence of past genocidal deeds?
For to do so, a growing ignorance feeds.

Tragically, for many of my kin, there is no marked grave.
The surviving few endured so much and were ever so brave.

The only memorial marker is our collective memory.
Why this important fact do some not seem to see?

To refuse to say the "genocide" word denies some form of closure.
A moral lapse for trade and commerce sadly comes to exposure.

I do not appreciate a bureaucratic memo or decree.
Why this important existential fact can't they see?

I reflect on the painful memory of my family and kin,
and wonder why some cannot acknowledge this dreadful sin.

Memory:

To be cursed by the memory of the genocide
is also to be blessed by the consciousness.

To suffer enduring pain
is to remember without fail.

To be a victim
is to discern what should be done.

To suffer
eventually leads to love.

To learn of our humanity,
to share our vulnerability,
to cry and to care,
and after a while to wipe our tears,
and finally to love another.

The memory of a harsh blow by a clenched fist and hard heart
leads us to seek a gentle caressing touch.

I remember the hated deeds,
yet I willingly turn to love.

I am transformed
into us.

Remembering Genocide:

We must remember.
Remember and learn.
Remember and tell.
But also remember and live.
And some day, remember and forgive.

Ancestral Voices:

Our ancestral voices,
flow as streams,
into the great ocean.

Where past, present and future,
rise and fall,
ebb and flow,
with the currents and tides
and prevailing winds.

Our ancestral voices
become a sea of endless waves
in a vast ocean
that stretches as far as the eye can see
and the mind can imagine.

* inspired by a Sheila Chandra song

Appendix I:
Selective Chronology of Headlines on the Armenian Genocide in Canadian Newspapers from 1915

From *L'Action Catholique*, (Quebec), jeudi 23 mars 1915
Sivas est brulée par les turcs: des milliers d'arméniens et de grecs y sont menacés

From *L'Action Catholique* (Quebec), mardi 8 août 1915
Les massacres en Arménie: nouveaux témoignages sur la barbarie des Jeunes-Turcs

From *La Patrie* (Quebec), samedi 25 septembre 1915
Le martyre d'une race: les Turcs poursuivent avec un esprit diabolique la destruction de la famille arménienne en détruisant ses villages

From *Le Devoir*, jeudi 7 octobre 1915
Arméniens massacrés: le vicomte Bryce estime à 800,000 le nombre des vctimes en Arménie—l'extermination est voulue et preméditée par le gouvernement turc

From *The Globe* (Toronto), Thursday, August 26, 1915
Turks slay 14,000 in one massacre: blackest page in Ottoman history revealed by former Italian Consul

From the *London Evening Free Press*, Thursday, September 23, 1915
Slaughter of Armenians is growing worse: tales of horror are laid before United States government at Washington

From *The Globe*, Friday, September 24, 1915
Terrible tales told of Turkish massacres: Armenian men systematically murdered—extermination the watchword

From the *Manitoba Free Press*, Saturday, September 25, 1915

Appalling story of Turk massacres: appeal made to United States to save Armenians from extinction

From the *Ottawa Evening Journal*, Saturday, September 25, 1915
Armenian mothers throw children in Euphrates to escape Turk torture: Turks exterminating Christians of the Empire by sending them into the desert where tribesmen starve, and kill them at leisure.

From the *St. Catherines Standard,* Thursday, October 7, 1915
Killed more Armenians in 3 days than did Abdul Hamid in 30 years: Enver Pasha proudly boasts that he has outdone the 'Red Sultan'—several once prosperous villages now devoid of any sign of life

From the *Toronto Daily Star*, Thursday, October 7, 1915
Threw 10,000 people into the sea to perish: Turks have practically wiped out the entire people of Armenia

From the *Ottawa Evening Journal*, Monday, November 29, 1915
Saturnalia of slaughter by refined methods as young Turks set out to wipe Armenian race off the world

From the *Berlin Daily Telegraph* (Ontario), Wednesday, December 15, 1915
Awful massacre of Armenians: worst stories of atrocities are confirmed by U. S. committee

From the *Toronto World*, Tuesday, December 21, 1915
Turks in Adrianople massacre Armenians: all have either been butchered or deported from the city

Appendix II:
Statement from the Association of Genocide Scholars

Association of Genocide Scholars

Department of Government
College of William and Mary
Williamsburg, Virginia 23187-8795 USA
757/221-3038, Fax 757/221-1868

Executive Board
Roger W. Smith, President
Frank Chalk, Vice President
Jack Nusen Porter, Vice President
Steven L. Jacobs, Treasurer

The Armenian Genocide Resolution Unanimously Passed By TheAssociation of Genocide Scholars of North America

The Armenian Genocide Resolution was unanimously passed at the Association of Genocide Scholars' conference in Montreal on June 13, 1997.

Resolution

That this assembly of the Association of Genocide Scholars in its conference held in Montreal, June 11-13, 1997, reaffirms that the mass murder of over a million Armenians in Turkey in 1915 is a case of genocide which conforms to the statutes of the United Nations Convention on the Prevention and Punishment of Genocide. It further condemns the denial of the Armenian Genocide by the Turkish government and its official and unofficial agents and supporters.

Among the prominent scholars who supported the resolution were: Roger W. Smith (College of William & Mary; President of AGS); Israel Charny (Hebrew University, Jerusalem); Helen Fein, Past President AGS); Frank Chalk (Concordia University, Montreal); Ben Kiernan (Yale University); Anthony Oberschall (University of North Carolina, Chapel Hill); Mark Levene (Warwick University, UK); Rhoda Howard (McMaster University, Canada), Michael Freeman (Essex University, UK), Gunnar Heinsohn (Bremen University, Germany)

The Association of Genocide scholars is an international interdisciplinary, non-partisan organization dedicated to the understanding and prevention of Genocide. The Association is an affiliate of The Institute For the Study of Genocide, New York, Dr. Helen Fein, Executive Director.

Appendix III:
Letter from Alan Whitehorn to the *Globe and Mail*

January 3, 1999.

Editor
The Globe and Mail
444 Front St., West
Toronto, Ontario M5V 2S9.

Dear Globe,

In reference to Liberal M.P. Julian Reed's questioning of whether or not there was a genocide of Armenians in Turkey during 1915 (*National Post*, February 24, 1999), I suggest Mr. Reed take time out from his duties as Parliamentary Secretary to the Minister of Foreign Affairs and go no further than the Library of Parliament archives where a simple reading of the Canadian newspapers of the day (most notably the Toronto *Globe*) provide the following verbatim headlines and editorials:

"Armenians Massacred in Hundred Villages" (May 24)
"Turks Slay 14,000 in One Massacre" (August 26)
"Armenian Refugees Declare That 70,000 Armenians Have Been Massacred" (September 9)
"Turk's Fall to End Campaign of Murder: Terrible Atrocities are Committed in the Near East" (September 16)
"The Cup of Turkey's Iniquity Full" (*Globe* editorial, September 22)
"Armenians Rescued From Pursuing Turks: French Cruisers Go to Help the Refugees" (September 23)
"Terrible Tales Told of Turkish Massacres: Armenian Men Systematically Murdered—Extermination the Watchword" (September 24)
"Million Armenians Wiped Out by Turks: Only 200,000 Armenian Inhabitants of Turkey Now Remain in Country" (October 23)

"No British Agents Fomenting Armenians: Massacres of Unsurpassing Horror Committed By Turks" (November 27)
"Armenia: The Unspeakable Tragedy" (*Globe* editorial, December 2)
"Million Armenians Massacred by Turks: Lord Bryce Publishes Further Report of Atrocities in Asia Minor" (December 15).

I look forward to Mr. Reed's explanations of these Canadian headlines and books by foreign diplomats and clergy present at the time in Turkey. To assist Mr. Reed, perhaps the *Globe* editors might be gracious enough to reprint one of the historic pages from the *Globe*.

Yours sincerely,
Alan Whitehorn

Appendix IV:
Letter from Lorne Shirinian to the *Toronto Star*

The Toronto Star, Thursday, July 15, 1999. A23.

Armenian genocide isn't just an allegation

Re: the Opinion page article, *Freedom Fighters, or Terrorists?* (July 4). The author, Harry Sterling, we are informed, is a retired Canadian diplomat formerly posted to Turkey.

As a Canadian, born in this country of Armenian heritage, and as a professor, a researcher in the field of Armenian studies and a writer, I am disappointed to see that the kind of cold war language and genocide denial rhetoric that appeared in his article still makes its way into our newspapers in contemporary news items.

Sterling refers to Armenians who may have "seemingly just causes," and who have taken revenge "for perceived historical grievances." The need to make known the deportation and slaughter of more than 1 million Armenians in 1915-16 is not a "seemingly" just cause. It is a most just cause.

Anyone who has studied the eyewitness sources and archival evidence found in the U. S. government archives, the British archives, and now most astonishingly in the German archives, as Germany was Turkey's ally during World War I, will understand that what the Turkish government did to its Armenian population was genocide.

To add misinformation to insult, Sterling states that "To this day, Armenians regularly try to assassinate Turkish diplomats."

I am not aware of any Armenian terrorist activity since 1990.

Perhaps Sterling gets his information from the Turkish embassy. Surely such contentious statements require references.

Finally, using the language of genocide deniers, Sterling calls the Armenian genocide "alleged." Half of the Armenian nation disappeared during World War I.

Both my parents were orphaned as very young children. All their families on both sides were killed.

Every Armenian family suffered terrible losses. This is not "alleged;" it is fact.

Anyone who reads the sources will understand the terrible wrong that was done to the Armenian people.

After a federal government committee studied the Armenian genocide, it made an announcement in the House of Commons on June 10 this year. Julian Reed, the parliamentary secretary for Minister of Foreign Affairs Lloyd Axworthy, read the Canadian government's position:

"On behalf of the minister of foreign affairs, I wish to inform the House that together with all Canadians we remember the calamity afflicted on the Armenian people in 1915. This tragedy was committed with the intent to destroy a national group in which hundreds of thousands of Armenians were subject to atrocities, which included massive deportations and massacres. May the memory of this period contribute to healing wounds as well as to the reconciliation of present-day nations and communities and remind us all of our collective duty to work together toward world peace."

Genocide—from Armenia to Kosovo—must be exposed and halted.

Lorne Shirinian,
Kingston.

Selected Bibliography on the Armenian Genocide

Books

Apramian, Jack. *The Georgetown Boys*, Second Edition. Hamilton: n.p., 1983.

Archives du génocide des arméniens: recueil de documents diplomatiques allemands extraits de 'Deutschland und Armenien (1914-1918)' par le Docteur Johannes Lepsius. Translated from German by Marie-France Letenoux. Paris: Fayard, 1986.

Baghdjian, Kevork K. *La confiscation, par le gouvernement turc, des biens arméniens...dits "abandonnés."* Montreal: n.p. 1987.

Bardakjian, Kevork. *Hitler and the Armenian Genocide.* Cambridge and Toronto: The Zoryan Institute, 1985.

Barton, James L. *Story of Near East Relief (1915-1930): An Interpretation.* New York: The Macmillan Company, 1930.

Bedoukian, Kerop. *The Urchin: An Armenian's Escape.* London: John Murray, 1978.

Bournoutian, George. *A History of the Armenian People, Volume II: 1500 A.D. to the Present.* Costa Mesa, CA: Mazda Publishers, 1994.

Bryce, Viscount. *The Treatment of the Armenians in the Ottoman Empire 1915-16, Documents Presented to Secretary of State for Foreign Affairs*, Second Edition. Beirut: Doniguian and Sons, 1979.

Chaliand Gérard and Yves Ternon, *The Armenians from Genocide to Resistance.* Translated by Tony Berrett. London: Zed Books, 1983.

Chichekian, Garo. *The Armenian Community of Québec.* Montreal: n.p., 1989.

Dadrian, Vahakn. *The History of the Armenian Genocide: Ethnic Conflict from the Balkans to the Caucasus.* Providence: Berghahn Books, 1995.

———. *Warrant for Genocide: Key Elements of Turko-Armenian Conflict.* New Brunswick, NJ: Transaction Publishers, 1999.

———. *Key Elements in the Denial of the Armenian Genocide: A Case Study of Distortion and Falsification.* The Zoryan Institute: Toronto and Cambridge, MA: 1999.

Davis, Leslie A. *The Slaughterhouse Province: An American Diplomat's Report on the Armenian Genocide, 1915-1917.* Edited by Susan K. Blair. New Rochelle, NY: Aristide D. Caratzas, 1989.

Etmekjian, James. *The French Influence on the Western Armenian Renaissance 1843-1915.* New York: Twayne Publishers, Inc., 1964.

Housepian Dobkin, Marjorie. *Smyrna 1922: The Destruction of a City.* Kent, Ohio: Kent State University Press, 1988.

Hovannisian, Richard. *Armenia on the Road to Independence 1918.* Berkeley and Los Angeles: University of California Press, 1969.

Kerr, Stanley E. *The Lions of Marash: Personal Experiences with American Near East Relief, 1919-1920.* Albany: Statue University of New York Press, 1973.

Kuper, Leo. *Genocide: Its Political Use in the Twentieth Century*. New Haven: Yale University Press, 1981.

Libaridian, Gerard. compiler. *The Armenian Genocide in the Canadian Press, Volume I, 1915-1916*. Montreal: Armenian National Committee, 1985.

Marashlian, Levon. *Politics and Demography: Armenians, Turks, and Kurds in the Ottoman Empire*. Toronto and Cambridge: The Zoryan Institute, 1991.

Memoirs of Naim Bey. Turkish Official Documents Related to the Deportations and Massacres of Armenians. Compiled by Aram Andonian. London: n.p., 1920. 43-44.

Miller Donald E. and Lorna Touryan Miller. *Survivors: An Oral History of the Armenian Genocide*. Berkeley and Los Angeles: University of California Press, 1993.

Mirak, Robert. *Torn Between Two Lands: Armenians in America, 1890 to World War I*. Cambridge: Harvard University Press, 1983.

Morgenthau, Henry. *Ambassador Morgenthau's Story*. Plandome, New York: New Age Publishers, 1975.

Nalbandian, Louise. *The Armenian Revolutionary Movement: The Development of Armenian Political Parties through the Nineteenth Century*. Berkeley and Los Angeles: University of California Press, 1967.

Nogales, Rafael de. *Four Years Beneath the Crescent*. Translated by Muna Lee, New York, 1926.

Riggs, Henry H. *Days of Tragedy in Armenia: Personal Experiences in Harpoot 1915-1917*. Ann Arbor: Gomidas Institute, 1997.

Shirinian, Lorne. *The Impact of the Armenian Genocide: Eighty-Three Years of Survival and Memory in the Armenian Diaspora*. Lectures and Papers in Ethnicity No. 27, December 1997. Robert F. Harney Professorship and Program in Ethnic Immigration and Pluralism Studies. Toronto: University of Toronto, 1997.

———. *Survivor Memoirs of the Armenian Genocide*. Reading, England: Taderon Press, 1999.

———. *Quest for Closure: The Armenian Genocide and the Search for Justice in Canada*. Kingston: Blue Heron Press, 2000.

Walker Christopher. *Armenia: The Survival of a Nation*. New York: St. Martin's Press, 1990.

Articles

Apramian, Jack. "The Georgetown Boys," in *Polyphony: The Bulletin of the Multicultural History Society of Ontario, Armenians in Ontario* 4.2 (Fall/Winter 1982): 43-52.

Boyajian, Levon and Haigaz Grigorian, "Psychosocial Sequelae of the Armenian Genocide," in *The Armenian Perspective*, edited by Richard Hovannisian. New Brunswick, NJ: Transaction Books, 1986. 177-185.

Charny, Israel. "A Contribution to the Psychology of Denial of Genocide," *Genocide and Human Rights: Lessons from the Armenian Experience*. A Special Issue of the *Journal of Armenian Studies* 4.1-2 (1992): 289-306.

Hofmann, Tessa. "German Eyewitness Reports of the Genocide of the Armenians, 1915-16," in The Permanent People's Tribunal. *Crime of Silence: The Armenian Genocide*. London: Zed Books, Ltd., 1985. 61-92.

Hofmann, Tessa and Gerayer Koutcharian. " 'Images that Horrify and Indict': Pictorial Documents on the Persecution and Extermination of the Armenians from 1877 to 1922," *Armenian Review* 45.1-2/177 (Spring-Summer 1992): 53-184.

Hovannisian, Anush. "Turkey: A Cultural Genocide," in *Problems of Genocide: Proceedings of the International Conference on 'Problems of Genocide' April 21-23, National Academy of Sciences, Yerevan, Armenia.* Toronto and Cambridge, MA: The Zoryan Institute, 1997. 376-385.

Kaprielian, Isabel. "Armenians in Ontario," *Polyphony* 4.2 (Fall/Winter 1982): 6-11.

Kouymjian, Dickran. "The Destruction of Armenian Historical Monuments as a Continuation of the Turkish Policy of Genocide," in The Permanent People's Tribunal. *A Crime of Silence.* London: Zed Books, 1985. 173-185.

———. "Confiscation and Destruction: A Manifestation of the Genocidal Process," *Armenian Forum* 3 (Autumn 1998): 1-12.

Moranian, Suzanne, Elizabeth. "Bearing Witness: The Missionary Archives as Evidence of the Armenian Genocide," in *The Armenian Genocide: History, Politics, Ethics,* Edited by Richard Hovannisian New York: St. Martin's Press, 1992. 103-128.

Nahabedian, Reverend Harold J. "A Brief Look at Relations between Canadians and Armenians, 1896-1920." *Polyphony* 4.2 (Fall/Winter 1982): 28-34.

Smith, Roger, Erik Markusen, and Robert J. Lifton. "Professional Ethics and the Denial of the Armenian Genocide," in *Remembrance and Denial: The Case of the Armenian Genocide*, edited by Richard Hovannisian. Detroit: Wayne State University Press, 1999. 271-295.

Staub, Ervin. "The Genocide of the Armenians: Psychological and Cultural Roots and the Impact on Survivors." *Armenian Review* 42.4/168 (Winter 1989): 55-70.

———. "Preventing Genocide: Activating Bystanders, Helping Victims Heal and the Creation of Caring," in *Problems of Genocide: Proceedings of the International Conference on 'Problems of Genocide' April 21-23, National Academy of Sciences, Yerevan, Armenia.* Toronto and Cambridge, MA: The Zoryan Institute, 1997. 386-397.

Ternon, Yves. "The State's Crime: On the Subject of the Armenian and the Jewish Genocides." *Genocide and Human Rights: Lessons from the Armenian Experience.* A Special Issue of the *Journal of Armenian Studies* 4.1-2 (1992): 97-108.

Van Boven, Théo "Paragraph 30: Note on the Deleted Reference to the Massacre of the Armenians in the Study on the Question of the Prevention and the Punishment of the Crime of Genocide," in The Permanent People's Tribunal. *A Crime of Silence: The Armenian Genocide.* London: Zed Books, 1985. 168-172.

BEHAVIOR THERAPY: A CLINICAL INTRODUCTION

Richard I. Lanyon
Arizona State University

and

Barbara P. Lanyon
Psychological Counseling Services
Scottsdale, Arizona

ADDISON-WESLEY PUBLISHING COMPANY

Reading, Massachusetts
Menlo Park, California
London • Amsterdam
Don Mills, Ontario • Sydney

616 .8914 L296b c. 1

Lanyon, Richard I., 1937–

Behavior therapy, a clinical introduction /

This book is in the
ADDISON-WESLEY SERIES
IN CLINICAL AND
PROFESSIONAL PSYCHOLOGY

Leonard D. Goodstein
Series Editor

Copyright © 1978 by Addison-Wesley Publishing Company, Inc. Philippines copyright 1978 by Addison-Wesley Publishing Company, Inc.

All rights reserved. No part of this publication may be reproduced, stored in a retrieval system, or transmitted, in any form or by any means, electronic, mechanical, photocopying, recording, or otherwise, without the prior written permission of the publisher. Printed in the United States of America. Published simultaneously in Canada. Library of Congress Catalog Card No. 77-83022.

ISBN 0-201-04100-6
BCDEFGHIJ-D0-79